A Good Walk Home

A Parable on Living and Dying Well

Larry Walkemeyer

A Good Walk Home, A Parable on Living and Dying Well

ALDERSGATE PRESS
THE PUBLICATIONS ARM OF
HolinessAndUnity.org

In Collaboration with
EMETH PRESS
www.emethpress.com
Lexington, Kentucky

Library of Congress Cataloging-in-Publication Data

Walkemeyer, Larry.
  A good walk home : a parable on living and dying well / Larry Walkemeyer.
      pages cm
  Includes bibliographical references and index.
  ISBN 978-1-60947-064-7 (alk. paper)
  1. Jesus Christ--Seven last words--Miscellanea. I. Title.
  BT457.W35 2013
  232.96'35--dc23
                    2013034779

Tracy Garner (tracygarner@charter.net) is the illustrator
who created the art design for the cover and interior

Map of the Journey

Preface

Dying is the reality we all would like to deny or at least delay. Yet birth and death define our humanness. They transcend all other distinctions that may divide us.

We do not prepare for birth; we are simply propelled into the reality of human life. None of us chooses our birthday, our birthplace, or our birth family.

Death is different. We generally have no control over our death day. But we do have considerable influence over how we journey toward death. Our decisions about how we will die can shape the quality of our death.

Most individuals, however, have no desire to learn the art of dying. Most live in an eyes-shut denial of death. Others keep it at arm's length rather than embracing it. Those who deal honestly with death often lack wisdom or personal role models. Few people know how to say a "great good-bye." Only a handful of people know how to take a good walk home. We are in debt to people like Elisabeth Kübler-Ross who have given us important insights for the journey of grief and death.

Jesus, the Great One, taught us how to live and what to believe about death. But did He specifically teach us how to journey toward death? Since his life teaches us how to live, might not his death instruct us about how to die?

On the day of his death, Jesus took a world-altering trek. His sacred expedition provided everything we would need for life and death. He died for us—but in his passion, Jesus was not only dying *for* us, but also teaching us *how* to die. On that final day, Jesus gave an invitation: "Watch how I walk home."

Jesus' death is punctuated by seven final sayings. Each saying comes in response to a challenge, an opportunity, or a desire. It is in these seven scenes that we learn how to die well and how to say a great good-bye.

In a world that seeks to escape, ignore or romanticize the reality of death, we are left untaught about the necessary steps for a healthy, holy journey home. Jesus' way of facing death imparts the essential wisdom that can transform the pain of death into an enduring legacy of love.

Our lives are stories penned by our decisions. Hearing a good story about an intensely personal subject can often assist us with our autobiographies. Sometimes a simple story can open the eyes of the heart to the most profound lessons in life. The following allegory offers signposts for traveling wisely through the valley of the shadow of death.

Although some readers don't yet know the final hope this story imparts, there is benefit for everyone in becoming familiar with the landscape of death. Almost all of us will have the honor of helping someone travel toward death. These lessons can equip us to be more helpful guides to those on the journey. The best map available is the holy journey to Reunion River.

When one is wisely and well-prepared for death, then all the best of life lies ahead. The following story is for those who want to live fully, even if it seems that their finish line is still far distant.

Prologue

Shadow Valley

"There is nothing more we can do for him"

At the sound of my doctor's words, my mind silently screamed. I rejected the death sentence. Surely the words were a bad dream induced by the pain meds dripping into my arm and traveling to my brain.

Let me sleep. Let me wake up again. Someone shake me!

But there stood Ann with our kids and my brother, Mike. The doctor's consoling arm around my tearful wife's shoulder was an undeniable exclamation point to the news he had delivered. The kids were holding each other. Mike was staring at the ceiling as if to single-handedly change the mind of God.

Something had gone terribly wrong! I had been given assurance that my heart could be fixed, that it was serious, but nothing surgery couldn't solve.

I wasn't young, but I wasn't old either, certainly not old enough to be finished with life.

Yes, I had started reading the obituaries and noting the ages of those who had passed. I took comfort in those older than me and wrote off those younger as anomalies. My lifestyle choices gave me high scores on the online longevity tests I'd taken. I was ahead of the curve.

Death. Of course I had thought about it. I was a smart guy and a religious guy. I had attended my share of funerals. But death was always on a distant horizon for me, never knocking at my door. With medicine being what it is, and the power of prayer being what it is, there was always something that could be done to keep the grim reaper in the waiting room But now . . . death was standing by my bed, calling my name.

Death. I didn't know how to die. I had a good handle on life and had done okay with my years. I made a living solving problems, mapping out strategies to conquer challenges. When tough stuff happened, the answer was, "Call Morty, he'll know what to do." But this was the ultimate challenge. I was totally out of my league and I knew it. I was mortified.

Death. I lay there and tried to bring clarity to my fuzzy thoughts. Just minutes ago, the room had been filled with cascading sunlight from a large picture window. But with the prognosis came a dark cloud to hide the sun, as if someone had drawn the blinds. The gloom matched my mood.

The silence of my mouth did not match the screaming of my mind.

Perhaps in my post-anesthesia stupor I had misinterpreted the entire scene. I tried calling out to God. *Father... Father...* but I could not lift the words higher than the stark white ceiling. My prayer thoughts bounced and rebounded to the bed.

Where was the power of my faith when I needed it? I tried again. *God, I feel trapped. I need your help! I want to live and I don't know how to die.* But there was a "gone to lunch" sign on the door of heaven, or so it seemed. I felt nothing but a toxic mix of desperation and frustration.

Although my mind tossed and turned, I felt my body drifting into a drug-induced slumber. On one hand, I welcomed an escape from the emotional anguish I felt. On the other, I dreaded sleep for fear I would never wake again.

The prayer I first learned kneeling with my mom and sister beside my bed came floating into my mind. *Now I lay me down to sleep, I pray the Lord my soul to keep. If I should die before I wake, I pray the Lord my soul to take.* Mentally repeating the words seemed mechanical, yet it was all I could think to do as I faced this journey of death. After a few recitations, I sank into a heavy sleep.

With no clue how long I had slept, I started awake in a very strange place. My slumber had transported me from the dim hospital room to a vast, dark valley. The first thing I noticed were the ominous clouds and shadows which crowded out the light from one end of the valley to the other.

The gorge was flanked by steep walls, created by sheer faces of rock—it reminded me of a narrow Grand Canyon, without the river at the floor.

The valley stretched before my vantage point: a clearing about the size of a football field, surrounded on all sides by a forbidding grove of impenetrable trees. It was a strange place, yet there were glimmers of familiarity. I couldn't put my finger on why, but it was not completely foreign to me. At the same time, the sight of that valley sent silent shivers of fear down my spine.

"Morty, wake up!" I shouted, trying to free myself from what could only be a bad dream. I slapped my face, pinched my arms, jumped up and down on one leg and even plucked my nostril hairs. But the valley remained— large and lonely, with no sign of life. At last, not sure what else to do, I sat down. Best to stay put until I woke up.

As I sat, terror began to rise like bitter bile. First, a death sentence. Now, a shadowy, sinister valley. *This has to be a nightmare*, I thought. But I could not recall ever feeling this consumed by fear in a dream.

I waited for what seemed like hours, neither sleeping nor waking. I was nearly numb, my mind moving as slow as molasses. I returned to one clear, overriding thought again and again: I wanted out, but there was no way out.

At last, I stood and began to shout in anger. "God, get me out of here now! What have I done to deserve this? Did I tick you off? I'm sorry. Let me out!"

Silence.

I yelled for a few more empty minutes. Only my Sunday school upbringing kept me from shaking my fist at the murky clouds above. Finally, the futility of my actions muzzled my ranting and I sank again to the ground.

Silence. Emptiness. Loneliness. Helplessness. Bitterness. This was the very bottom.

But then I heard them. At first it was faint, but even at a distance the sound was a vile *kee-eeee-arh*. The screeches were the cries of a child in pain mixed with a hoarse, hate-filled scream, each two to three seconds long, but seeming much longer. I scanned the sky for their source.

I saw nothing and had nearly I convinced myself I'd only imagined the sound. Just when I was settling into the comfort of this thought, I heard them again. Closer. Louder. Uglier.

Then I saw specks high in the sky, circling, some twenty of them. Wide circles at first, but narrowing with each revolution. Even at that height, it was obvious that I was the center point of their attention. I prayed they would not descend, but it was as if my fear was magnetic. With each circle they dropped by at least a hundred feet.

I wanted to jump to my feet and run, but my sorrow, confusion, and fear had become like sacks of cement tied to my limbs. I felt paralyzed.

They were about eighty feet above me when I was finally able to stand. Now I could clearly see the hawks: sleek, dark bodies with dark, ugly red tails. They soared effortlessly on broad wings, and their outstretched talons seemed to reach directly for my face. Razor-sharp beaks unhinged every few seconds to emit hideous, blood-curdling screeches that I tried to block with hands pressed over my ears.

They watched me for two or three minutes and I began to hope that they were only curious and tormenting, not actually dangerous. Then I noticed that the largest and most malicious hawk had fixed his eyes upon me. Suddenly, he tucked his wings and swooped down, screaming its vile screech. I threw up my hands and ducked. Talons missed by only a few feet.

This first move released the others to attack. One by one they dove toward me, each closer than the last. I tried to run, only to stumble over my own leaden feet. As I fell, a talon sliced across my outstretched forearm.

They would finish me now, I knew. In desperation I cried, "Jesus, Jesus, Jesus!" It was something I'd heard my wife do when it seemed we were in imminent danger. Once, black ice had whipped our car into 360-degree spins at seventy miles an hour. Her cries seemed to stop the car as if by magic.

I believed in prayer, but it was something I usually turned to only after the rest of my efforts had failed. I was at that point now, absolutely helpless. With all the strength I could muster, I screamed again, "Jesus, Jesus, Jesus!"

The hawks screeched in unison and dove toward me. I closed my eyes in anticipation of their beaks and talons. But then their cries changed. What had been the menacing sound of torment now sounded like barnyard hens clucking in fear as they were scattered before the farmwife's broom.

When I opened my eyes, I saw an older man striding confidently across the clearing, his walking stick held high above his head. The hawks scattered in every direction, thrown into fear and chaos by his very appearance.

"*Hola*, amigo! I've been watching you," he called while still a distance away. His was a lilting voice, warmth and strength blending in its deep rich tones.

I was so relieved to be free from the birds that I wanted to hug my liberator. At the same time, I felt like snapping, "Watching me this whole time? Thanks a lot! Were you just going to stay in the woods and watch me die?"

In this conflicted state, I stood in open-mouthed silence. I knew I was staring, but the combination of gratitude, curiosity, and frustration rendered me speechless and impolite.

As the man came closer, I saw he was a distinguished, older Latino man. His shoulder-length gray hair was pulled into a neat ponytail at his neck. A toothy, bright smile contrasted richly with his golden brown skin. His eyes seemed to dance with a mixture of contentment and excitement. In one hand he carried a large stick which he used like a walking cane. The overall effect of his appearance was strongly and strangely comforting.

"Where are you headed?" he inquired sincerely.

"Anywhere but here," I quipped back, immediately regretting my smart mouth. Then, I couldn't stop myself. I blurted my desperate emotions and questions: "Thank you, thank you, thank you! Who are you? Where am I? When can I get out of here? What's this all about? Where's my wife? Where's the doctor? Why am I dying?"

"Whoa, my friend. Let's take 'em one at a time if you don't mind. You're welcome. I am Manuel. You are in Shadow Valley. You are on a journey. I am not sure when it will be finished. You will find out what it's all about as you go along. And what were the other questions?" In a gesture of enthusiastic friendliness, he offered his open hand to me.

I hesitated, caught between caution and desire. Then I shook his hand. I was struck by how rough, yet soothing his grip was. Just his touch started to ratchet my anxiety down a few levels.

"What were those devil birds? They nearly killed me!" I exclaimed as I reluctantly let go of his solid, reassuring hand.

"We call those Hater Hawks. They abhor and attack anything I love," he replied with remorse in his eye.

"Well, I hope I never hear from them again," I said.

Manuel paused for a moment, then answered, "That is my desire too, but unfortunately I think that wish is a bit premature." He went on, "I didn't catch your name."

"My name's Morty and, no offense, but I'm in the middle of a really bad dream," I said.

Manuel replied with a smile. "Are you certain it's a dream? You appear fairly real to me."

"Right now I am not certain about anything except that I have no idea where

I am or what to do next."

"Perhaps there's something I can do for you," said Manuel.

"Thanks for what you've already done. But unless you can wake me up, I don't think there is anything you can do for me."

"Why not?"

Flashing back to the hospital room, I answered, "Because the doc says nothing more can be done for me. I am on death row, you understand? I am dying soon." I paused and then added, "If I haven't already."

Manuel chuckled, but without malice or condescension. It was a muted laugh of encouragement that seemed to say, "Maybe . . . maybe not." Then he cleared his throat, looked me deep in the eyes, and declared, "There is something that can be done, but no one can do it for you. You must decide to do it for yourself. If indeed you are dying, then I am here to watch how you do it."

My mind flashed back to the time I was caught in a bitterly cold rip tide off an island in the Pacific Northwest. The dingy which had been tied to our boat had come loose and I dived in to retrieve it. But the wind and current caught and whisked it away, leaving me struggling to stay afloat as I was dragged out to sea. A photographer on the island ran along the shore, snapping pictures of the scene as it unfolded. I could see him as I fought to free myself from the relentless current. When I finally, miraculously, made it back to shore, the photographer was disappointed. He said, "I thought I was watching you die. I was going to show it to the world."

I didn't need anyone to watch me die. I didn't want to die. I didn't know how to die. I turned to Manuel and retorted, "Thanks for the offer, but if I am dying I would rather do it alone. The last thing I need is an audience."

Manuel shot back, "While it is true that no one can do it for you, you also cannot do it on your own. Getting through this valley is tough, the hardest thing you will ever do. I can help you make it to the end of the valley."

"That's just the point; I don't want to go through the valley," I replied.

"Well," Manuel said, "that is where you have a choice. You can go through the valley or you can lie down and die right here. I will return to the woods and watch from a distance." Manuel paused, then continued. "But there's a lot you can gain from walking through the valley. And know this: I am not here to watch you like a spectator. I am here to watch you like a guardian watches over an expensive treasure."

I looked toward the end of the valley and thought deeply. I asked, "If I am going to die anyway, why should I care whether I die here or at the end of the valley?"

Manuel seemed ready for that question. "It's true that most people stop here. They lie down and whimper until their life expires. But a few take the journey and are rewarded with an experience that makes the trip more than worth the effort. I've been to the other end of the valley."

"Why did you come back? What are you doing here?"

"Many years ago I faced this valley for the first time, alone. Something amazing happened to me when I reached the end. After that journey, I promised myself I would offer my help to anyone who found himself or herself here. I've learned a lot about this place and am willing to guide you through it. But only if you really want my help."

I gazed once more at the ominous valley. It looked even darker at the far end than where I stood. But when I turned my gaze to Manuel's confident and inviting brown eyes, I said, "Well, I've always tried to be a man who did things well, a man of action more than someone just waiting. So we might as well at least walk that direction."

Without another word, Manuel turned around, staff in hand, and headed down the valley. I had to step lively to stay even a few steps behind the spry old man.

I had countless questions, but I felt too overwhelmed to speak. So I just walked for a while. My mind raced through the past few hours, back through my illness, back through my marriage, back through my childhood. My life had come to an end much too soon. As I mulled over the reality of death, I quickened my pace and pulled up beside Manuel. "Mind if I ask a question?"

"I welcome questions. Any questions," Manuel replied.

"Does this valley have a name?"

"It's called Shadow Valley," he answered. Then he smiled and quipped, "For obvious reasons."

"Is it very far to the end of valley?"

"Do you remember when you went on a summer vacation in your car and your kids would ask, 'Are we there yet?' To them the journey seemed like forever, but to you it seemed just the distance you knew it would be, the distance it was supposed to be. This journey is like that."

I wanted to ask how Manuel knew I had kids, but I grunted, "I see."

We reached a couple of rocks just the right size for sitting. I was a bit winded and was about to ask if we could take a break when Manuel said, "Why don't we sit for a spell?"

As we sat, I grew braver in my questioning. "Is death a friend or a foe? Should I welcome it or fight against it?"

Manuel looked into the distance and was silent for a long time. I wondered if he hadn't heard the question or was purposely ignoring me. But finally, in a low and reverent tone, he spoke. "Death is neither a friend to be embraced nor an enemy to be hated. It is a visitor whose persistent, troublesome knock must be answered. We open the door only to find the rude visitor gone and either light or darkness remaining. One day, the visitor's obnoxious knocking will be silenced forever."

He stopped and gazed upward for a few seconds. "The Great One was the first to walk this entire valley. He fought a great battle to ensure the knocking would someday cease."

I was confused about all I had just heard, including who the "Great One" was. But before I could ask, Manuel stood, reached behind the rock he had been sitting on, and pulled out a crimson backpack. He offered it to me and said, "My gift to you. You are going to want this."

"What's in it?" I inquired.

"All you need for the journey. Something for each stop along the way."

I took the backpack. It felt empty. I shook it and it sounded empty. "I think you forgot to fill it," I said.

Manuel laughed. "I like to fill it just in time, not ahead of time." Then he began to walk, ready to continue on our way.

I slipped on the backpack, tightened the straps, and hustled to catch up with my elderly guide. We were on our way . . . somewhere.

Stage 1

Reconciliation Rocks

"Forgive them for they know not what they do"

anuel and I walked side by side in silence for some time. The valley floor was level and grassy. Occasionally the path disappeared into a grove of tall trees, and I followed as Manuel weaved his way through the dense forest to the other side. I was certain I would have been hopelessly lost if I had been traveling alone.

As we journeyed forward, there was a comfortable silence between us. When we came through yet another confusing grove of trees, the valley floor changed dramatically at our feet. There was a rift in the ground, like the crevasses I had encountered when mountain climbing across glaciers. I guessed the chasm was eighty feet wide or so, bisecting the valley and

stretching from one side to the other. There was no avoiding it. You couldn't go around it. You couldn't go forward without crossing it.

This troubled me at first. But then, as we drew a bit closer, I saw that there was a bridge across the divide, with a sign identifying it as the Bridge of Forgiveness. I began to relax. This would be a simple jaunt across a narrow wooden bridge. No problem.

Manual led us toward it. As we arrived, I was struck by the depth of the divide. I couldn't see the bottom. The solid plank bridge looked to be about four feet wide, with latticework on both sides and sturdy handrails held up by posts every few feet. It seemed quite trustworthy and secure.

However, the bridge had one peculiar feature that puzzled and then worried me: the surface was covered with sharp, dark rocks of varying sizes and shapes. The smallest ones were the size of golf balls. The largest were the size of jagged oranges.

"This part of our journey is called Reconciliation Rocks," Manuel said as he bounded on to the bridge. He acted as if the rocks were smooth marbles, striding swiftly across without missing a beat. Then he turned and looked at me as if to say, "What are you waiting for?"

I took one careful step at a time across the bridge. "Ouch! Ooh! Ugh!" Each stride brought excruciating pain. My sturdy shoes were no defense against the razor-sharp rocks; they were soon sliced through in several spots. The jagged stones began to cut into my feet and I could feel warm blood oozing from the cuts. A quarter of the way across, I stopped and looked at Manuel.

"What now? I can't go any further! I'm stuck!" I shouted, hoping Manuel would skip back my direction and magically carry me across on his back.

"Yep, looks like those rocks are killing you!" yelled Manuel.

"What are these stupid rocks doing here anyway?" I inquired in disgust.

"You put them there, Morty! They are your rock collection."

"Why would I ever collect such ugly, jagged rocks?"

"Every person has a rock collection they need to get through," said Manuel. I watched from a distance as he bent down, picked up a stick and began to draw in the dirt at the end of the bridge. His actions were baffling, given my painful predicament. I couldn't go forward, backward, or even sit down. So I leaned over to make a closer examination of the source of my pain.

It was then that I noticed a most peculiar thing: each ragged stone was engraved with a name, the name of someone I knew. Sam, Peter, Tommy, ... Many of them were engraved with my own name, Morty. In smaller letters under each name were a few unkind words. "Worthless pig." "Why can't you be like your brother?" "Loser." "I wish you were never born!" "Fang face." "Hopeless Jerk." "Idiot." "I hate you!" These were words I had carelessly hurled at others in my lifetime, or that had been hurtfully thrown at me.

I thought of the liar who had first penned the children's rhyme, "Stick and stones will break my bones, but words will never hurt me." What a deception! Words can cut more deeply than stones any day. I realized how stuck I really was. If I couldn't deal with these stones I could never move forward.

"What do I do now?" I called to Manuel.

"First, take off your shoes!"

I shook my head in disbelief. "Are you crazy? My shoes didn't even protect me. Now you want me to go barefoot?"

"That's right. Trust me, I've been through the rocks many times; shoes won't help you!"

Feeling foolish and completely vulnerable, I removed my shoes, exposing my tender feet to the sharp stones. I stood absolutely still in an effort to minimize the pain. "Now what?"

"How about checking your backpack?" Manuel suggested.

I slid the crimson backpack off my back and reached inside. It felt empty at first, but then I felt something made of glass. When I withdrew my hand, I saw what looked like a small perfume bottle. Removing the cap, my nose was filled with a pungent scent. The aroma was sweet, yet very strong.

Manuel, who was watching from the far side of the chasm, called out, "It's called Grace Oil. If you are willing to release the people who have hurt you, and ready to request the forgiveness of those you have injured, it can help you."

I thought about some of the rocks that had been thrown at me. The people who double-crossed me, disappointed me, lied to me, betrayed me, attacked me unjustly. Did they really deserve forgiveness?

On the other hand, did I?

I looked at the Grace Oil in my hand. "Isn't grace about receiving what we don't deserve?" I said this looking at Manuel for some response. He just smiled, implying that the answer was obvious. I surely did not deserve what grace might provide.

Then it dawned on me that the people who had thrown those hateful words toward me didn't have a clue how sharp their missiles were. They hadn't known what they were doing. I certainly hadn't known how much damage would be done by the nasty words I'd thrown around.

I recalled the time my stepdad had slapped my thirteen-year-old face and said, "Where is your brain? You are going nowhere in life." Even now, remembering those words aroused in me emotions of anger and inadequacy. He hadn't realized that he was drawing a knife across my self-image that would leave an ugly scar for life. Although eventually I had forged a truce with my stepdad, I had never extended forgiveness to him.

My own hurtful words also flashed in my mind. I knew too well the times I had shot the canon of my tongue in the direction of someone who had angered me. Oh, the tongue! I had once been the ringleader of a writing campaign to see a certain professor removed from the college staff. His resignation was a personal triumph for me. Only later did I discover that most of the allegations I had used as ammo against him were the imaginings of an individual with a personal vendetta against him. The revelation came too late for his career. There, beneath my right foot, was a large rock with his name on it.

There was no way I could cross this bridge without Manuel's help. I called out, "I need your help! How do I get past these rocks?"

"Pour the oil on the rocks," he directed.

I began to drip a tiny bit of Grace Oil on each of the sharp stones.

"Don't dribble it, drench them!" Manuel yelled.

"But there won't be enough," I protested.

"You might be surprised," he said with a smile in his voice. There is always enough.

I tipped the bottle over and poured out the oil, calling the name printed on each rock. "I forgive you, Sam." "I forgive you, Joe." "Forgive me, Sandra!"

Two curious things happened. As oil splashed on the rocks, the jagged stones transformed to a surface smooth as a marble floor. Also, the bottle did not run dry; it spilled out more and more fragrant, healing oil. It seemed as though the more I poured, the more there was to pour. Grace is an amazing thing.

I wept as I called out each name and covered our spiteful words with oil. People who had failed me were blessed. People who had wronged me were released. People I had angered were honored. People I had judged were commended. Step by step, I crossed the Bridge of Forgiveness by generously pouring out Grace Oil.

When I took the final step, Manuel was there waiting with arms spread wide. "Bravo, my friend, bravo!" I awkwardly leaned into Manuel's arms and received a congratulatory hug.

Still hugging me, I heard him say, "Many people turn around at the bridge. It's simply too hard for them to cross over. They would rather remain stuck than share grace."

After the bear hug was done, I examined my feet. Where they had been bleeding, they were mysteriously healed. They were still a little swollen, but there were only large, ugly blue scars where the cuts had been.

I felt lighter, like a burden had been lifted off of my shoulders. I looked back at the bridge and felt an unexpected gratitude. Without this journey, I may have finished my life without ever administering the "oil of grace." I had a sense that this painful bridge was, ironically, the most healing place I had ever been.

Stage 2

Paradise Pond

"Today you shall be with me in Paradise"

Leaving the bridge behind us, Manuel and I trekked onward through the overcast valley. For some time we picked our way quietly through a dense forest, then broke suddenly into a large clearing. In the middle was a pond of water. It was filled with the brightest turquoise water I had ever laid eyes on. The surface was very still. It was breathtaking.

Ramrod-straight pine trees stood like noble soldiers protecting the clearing. Thick, dazzling green grass led like a welcome mat to the gently sloping bank. Adorning the edges of the pond were masses of pure white Easter lilies, blue-lavender morning glories, and stunning red roses. I caught my

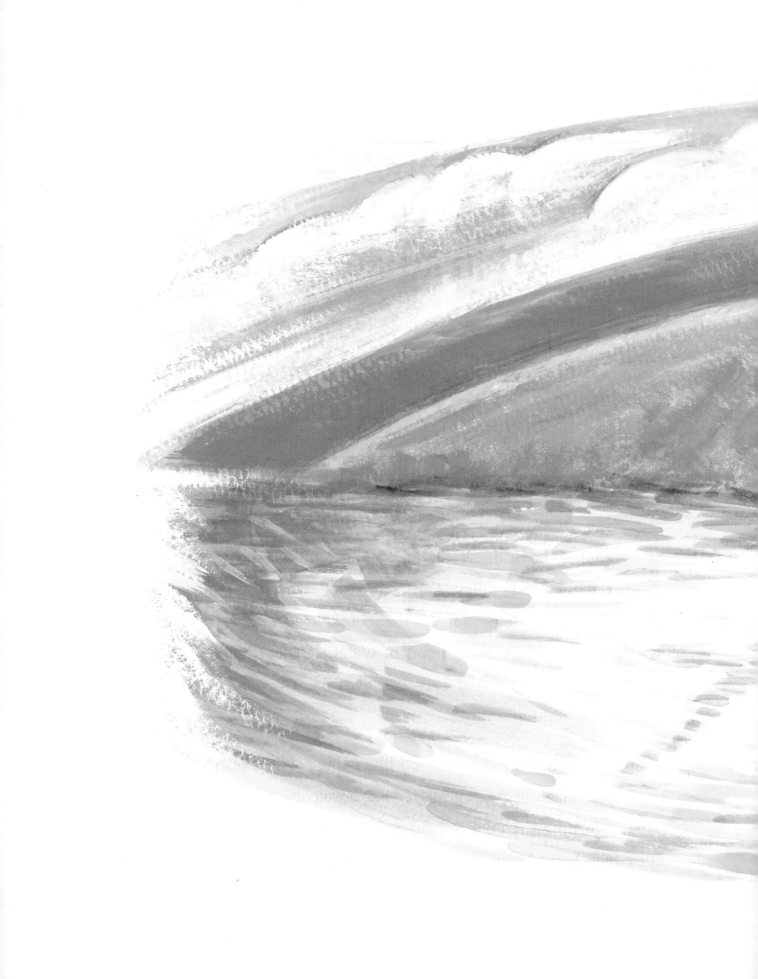

breath at the splendor of it all. I turned to Manuel and declared, "Amazing... simply amazing!"

"Not bad, huh? It's called Paradise Pond. It deserves a close look."

The pond had a magnetic quality that drew me to its water. I made my way to the edge and leaned over the reflective surface. I peered into the glassy water, then let out an abrupt scream of horror. The idyllic moment had been shattered by a nightmarish image reflected on the pond's surface.

It was my face . . . or, at least, a person who resembled me. The haunting countenance was ghastly. Deep-set, hollowed eyes rested atop sunken cheeks that had the pallor of death. I could almost see my skull showing through paper-thin skin marred by dark black blotches. My gums were pulled back to expose decaying teeth. The Halloween horror of the scene might have been less shocking had it not been so clearly my own face. It was as if I were seeing my ugliness, death, and hell mashed together.

"Am I dead?" I blurted in confusion and fear. I recoiled and fell onto the grass, trembling from what I had seen.

Manuel answered me with his own question. "What do you believe about life after death, Morty? Look again, deeper this time, right at the image in the water."

I didn't ever want to look at that scene again. I hesitated. Perhaps Manuel made his invitation because the next view would be different. If so, it might erase the horrific image that now dominated my mind.

So I took a chance. I leaned over the edge of the pond and gazed into the water again.

The image was even uglier and more vivid than the first time. But there was something different. This time I noticed the dark cloud which hung over the emaciated face. And then I saw *them* reflected in the water, and I heard their hideous cry: *kee-eeee-arh.* The Hater Hawks! Panic struck and I fell back from the water's edge, gasping for air. My eyes frantically searched the sky for the evil birds. It took several moments to realize they were nowhere in sight, and several more for my pulse to stop racing.

Manuel sat down beside me. He held a stunning red rose in his hands, and he peeled petals off, one by one, dropping them to the ground. After a few moments, he asked gently, "Horrible, huh?"

"Downright terrifying! I saw death, darkness, and those ugly hawks."

"Do you believe that is all there is?" Manuel asked. "Is there anything beyond what you can see? Do you believe that there is more past this life?"

I thought for a moment and said, "I have always told people I believe in heaven. I have had beautiful ideas about what it might be like. But it never felt right thinking too often or too deeply about an afterlife."

My mom had always sternly warned me of folks who were "too heavenly minded to be of any earthly good." I had certainly seen people I thought fit her description. They spent hours at church, hours in prayer meetings, hours studying the Bible, but they couldn't find a few minutes to help the needy next door to the church. But now I wondered if their problem was not that they thought too much of heaven, but that they thought too little of others. A truly "heavenly" mind surely would think up ways to make a difference on earth.

I guess I also felt that people used "paradise" as an excuse to commit acts of stupidity during this life. Blow up a bus with a bomb in your jacket and inherit your seventy-two virgins. Give your pension check to the televangelist to buy a new private jet and gain healing now and heavenly reward later. No doubt about it, "paradise" had been abused.

Frankly, my biggest block to thinking much about heaven was the nagging fact that you had to die to get there. It was more comforting just to keep my mind on earth, on the here and now. Imagining heaven was to admit death was real and just around the corner.

Heaven had never been real to me. I had a philosophy of heaven, but it certainly wasn't real enough to produce much comfort or motivation. I felt no anticipation for what seemed to be more fantasy than reality.

I looked into Manuel's eyes and sensed that he had somehow heard every thought. He said, "Morty, your vision is blocked. Your focus is on death instead of heaven. Your doubts are feeding your fears and robbing you of hope." He inclined his head toward the pond. "Dip your hand in the water."

He had to be joking. I was never going near that cursed, haunted pond again. I doubted that there was even water below its evil-mirror surface. It might be a pretend place of perfection that existed only in my wishes, but more likely was nothing but illusion and terror.

Manuel urged me forward. "Hey, you don't have to even look. Just stick your hand in. See if Paradise Pond is real."

Without looking, I dipped my hand beneath the water's surface. There was water down there after all. I pulled it out, dripping.

Manuel chuckled. "No mirage, is it? Looks pretty wet to me. Too many folks view heaven like some helpful figment of the imagination, some Disneyland in the sky. In fact, it is the most real destination there is. People would do well to meditate daily on its reality and reward. But it's a somewhat exclusive place."

"What do you mean?" I asked.

"Most people assume that they will end up there. But that's a very dangerous assumption." He stopped talking, and I saw an emotional tremor welling up in his eyes. Stray tears silently trickled down the wrinkles of his weathered cheeks. He seemed to choke back an anguished grief, lest he break into uncontrolled sobbing.

For a moment I forgot my own pain and felt compelled to comfort him, but no words came. His grief seemed too monumental for me to risk uttering a few trite words. All I could do was stare off in the distance and wait.

When I finally looked back to Manuel, he still held the rose in his hands, but now no petals remained. He gazed in mourning at the empty stem and finally spoke. "Created for such beauty, robbed of their glory. So many people will be met with a terrifying surprise. It's all so unnecessary, Morty."

We sat in silence for a few minutes as Manuel regained his composure. I wondered about my own life. Was Manuel saying something about me? Had I assumed something that I had no right to assume? Was I confident in what I believed? What did I really trust in?

Manuel interrupted my thoughts, "I think you should look in the water again."

"I don't think so!" I shot back.

"I understand your reluctance, Morty. Perhaps if you checked your backpack first," he suggested.

Remembering the Grace Oil, I reached into the backpack, anxious to see what magic could be waiting there. At first I felt nothing, but then my hand rested on two rough sticks. I withdrew them. They were coarse, with splinters protruding. One was about twenty-four inches in length, the other about ten. I had no idea what they could be.

"Pioneer sticks," Manuel said, answering my unspoken question.

"Weird name. What are they for?"

"When you cross them, they change everything they touch."

"Really?" I was dubious. "What about the name?"

"Someone had to be the first to pioneer the path to Paradise Pond. The 'Great One' blazed the trail on two pieces of wood," he answered. "Cross them and place them in the water."

Of course, I thought. This is where my confidence must come from. This is what can drive my doubts away. Courage and assurance began to rise in my chest.

With the two sticks crossed, I placed them in the water, plunging them beneath the surface that earlier had reflected only death. Trembling from my first two water visions, I still avoided gazing into the water.

"Now look again and tell me what you see," Manuel urged.

Did I really believe the pioneer sticks would change things? Daring to trust Manuel's words and the power of the crossed sticks, I leaned over to stare once more at the water.

The ghostly, ghastly visage was gone. The Hater Hawks were nowhere to be seen. On the water's smooth surface, I saw brilliant blue skies punctuated by fluffy white clouds. Sunbeams emanated through the holes in the clouds. I glanced up from the water to look at the sky. It was as dark and foreboding as it had been a few minutes ago. Yet, when I looked at the water again, sun-filled skies filled my vision.

It was like looking into a giant TV screen. Every color on earth, and some I had never seen before, danced across the surface of the water. On one edge of the scene, a pristine waterfall cascaded over a lush tropical hillside. On the other edge was a splendid banquet table set with the finest silver, gold, and china. The food that filled the table looked so appealing that I almost reached into the water to grasp it.

Against this astonishing backdrop, my face came into view, only this time it was bursting with health and vitality. It was the face of a robust thirty-year-old whose eyes danced with joy and peace. This reflection was as opposite from the first image as possibly could be imagined. It was true: the two sticks had somehow changed everything they touched.

As I stared, my feelings were both indescribable and uncontainable. I tried to connect my emotions with anything I had experienced on earth. The closest I could come was a feeling I'd had one Christmas Eve. That weekend a blizzard had hit as I was driving home from college. I had driven slowly all through the night, staying just ahead of road closures. About noon on Christmas Eve, I was only thirty miles from home when I ran off the deserted road. My car was stuck. I remember feeling hungry, exhausted, cold, and scared. It was the Christmas Eve from hell.

I had huddled in desperation, shivering in the car for a couple of hours without a single vehicle passing. Then it came to me that I should pray, so I began to talk to God. At first it was complaining, but then it turned to pleading. And then I began to sing. I sang every church song I could remember. As I was singing "Amazing Grace" for the third time, the headlights of a truck suddenly appeared in my window. I was rescued!

My rescuers lived a few farms down from ours and they delivered me right to my doorstep. Forever imprinted on my heart was the emotion of *being home*. I stepped into our huge family room, the aroma of turkey and pumpkin pie wafting through the air. The brilliant Christmas tree was festooned with the bright ornaments of my childhood, and shining gifts were piled high beneath its boughs. Bing Crosby's smooth baritone voice sang about "chestnuts roasting on an open fire" as family members laughed and hugged the stuffing out of me, saying, "Welcome home, Morty." I was safe, warm, and filled with deep peace. I was home.

Seeing my reflected face in Paradise Pond, I had that same feeling, but magnified many times.

After a few minutes the scene in the water began to fade. As it did, I noticed that something in me had changed. My grief-heavy heart, which had felt like a bowling ball in my chest, was light as a balloon. It floated and gave a joyful tug at the string that kept it tethered to earth. I longed to float heavenward and escape this dark valley. It was so real and so compelling that I stood to my feet and took a little leap to see if I could fly.

Manuel laughed aloud. "Trying to fly? You don't have wings yet, Morty! Why don't you put your feet in the water instead?"

I stepped into the pond. It was only one foot deep. I felt a surge of energy bolt through my body. "That's far enough," Manuel called. "Come back out."

I stepped out of the water with reluctance. As I did, I looked down at my feet, injured not long ago on the Bridge of Forgiveness. Where there had been swelling and scars from the rocks, now there was brand new skin, perfect as a baby's bottom. No age spots, no varicose veins, no wrinkles. They were strong and supple, new in every way.

I wanted to baptize my whole body in the pond. As if one step ahead of such an action, however, Manuel declared, "Not yet, Morty. This is the appetizer, not the meal. What did you see when you looked in the water this time?"

"I saw a glimpse of Paradise, Manuel, and with me in the middle of it!"

My guide snapped his finger rapidly, three times, pointed his finger at me and half shouted, "Remember it! Focus on it! Burn this Paradise image into your mind. You will need to keep that picture very clear as we continue our journey through Shadow Valley. When the darkness and heaviness press in on you, remind yourself of the reality you have seen. It will strengthen you."

I was ready to accept his advice, but surely was surprised by Manuel's next instruction. He said, "Look one last time into the pond."

Surprised or not, I was happy to comply. I expected to see the same glorious picture, but that's not what it was. When I peered at the glassy surface, the dark cloud had returned to the water. This time it was not my face that I saw. Instead, I saw the faces of people I cared about. Each was blindfolded.

As I gazed at the faces, I realized what they had in common. They were people who had no time for God. They were busy on earth with little concern for heaven. They were unprepared for Paradise. The euphoria I had been feeling was replaced by deep concern. How sad, all of these blinded people.

My cousin Benny's face was in the water. Next to him was my secretary's face, Rachel. I had tried to impact their lives. My life was dedicated to being a good example in the hope that one day they might ask me about my religious beliefs. But that never happened. I now realized that I should have been bolder.

Manuel knew what I saw, and even what I was feeling. He remarked, "As you travel from here to the end of Shadow Valley, Morty, you may have opportunity to share what you have seen today. You need to be ready to leverage your journey for the healing of the blindness of your friends. People are often captive audiences when they are watching you die."

I breathed a silent prayer for the faces I had seen, and then stood upright once more. I recalled my glimpse of glory and, sure enough, I felt a surge of strength. I knew I still had to walk the valley, but Paradise was a destination well worth the trip.

"I am ready, let's journey on, Manuel." I said this with new confidence. And so we moved on.

Stage 3

Friendship Field

"Woman, behold your son"

As we walked onward through the valley, I thought of all the sad goodbyes I would soon be forced to say. "Goodbye" is a strange word. I recalled that it had originated as an abbreviation of "God be with you." It was a word of blessing.

Soon I would have to say a final "God be with you . . . because I can no longer be with you." The thought saddened me. I believed God would be with my loved ones, but I wanted to be there too.

After passing through a dense section of tall shrubs, we broke into a lush, green meadow. Scattered throughout the clearing were flowers of vibrant colors and startling shapes. The sight was breathtaking. I paused to take it all in.

As I was gazing with admiration, several rabbits hopped slowly into the meadow. These were the most unusual rabbits I had ever laid eyes on. They were dazzling white, with floppy ears and small feet, and a variety of colorful markings on their faces. As they came closer, their bright eyes seemed to sparkle with love and friendliness.

As outlandish as it seems, one particular rabbit reminded me of my mom, Maria. Another resembled my best friend, Ted. A particularly small one reminded me of my kid sister, Lynn. Others looked like other friends and family members who were special to me. I shook my head and rubbed my eyes, but the likenesses remained. The rabbits looked at me with familiar, tender eyes.

I felt a sudden wave of yearning course through my body. I needed to be comforted. I needed companionship. I was tired of traveling this valley without the presence of those who were important to me. I knew I would feel so much better if only I could hold and cuddle these fluffy rabbits.

As I walked toward the closest bunny, however, it hopped away. This was unsettling. Because of the way it had looked at me, I thought it would jump right into my arms. I shrugged my shoulders and started toward the rabbit that reminded me of my sister. "Hey, little Lynn! It's okay, I need to hold you." But this rabbit also turned and hopped beyond my reach.

By now I was feeling desperately anxious and needy. *Don't these rabbits know I am a dying man? Don't they care? Can't they stop moving long enough to spend a little time with me?*

I dashed toward another rabbit, which ducked my grasp and hopped away. Again and again the scene repeated itself. I grew ever more desperate to capture a rabbit for myself.

Just when I need them most, they are distancing themselves from me, I thought. They were near me, yet unreachable, untouchable. How hurtful. Why?

After one more futile attempt, I stood in the middle of the field, panting from exhaustion, angry and confused. Finally, I looked at Manuel, who shook his head in sympathy and understanding. "Not very effective is it?" he said, stating the obvious.

"I don't get it!" I fumed. "They seem so friendly and so focused on me and so ready to hop into my arms, yet when I seek to catch them, they run."

"Do you really want to understand what's going on here, Morty?"

"Yes, I would love to know why I am being rejected like this," I retorted with more irritation than I intended.

"Then let me ask you a question. Do you have any people who are especially beautiful to you, people whom you long to have close to you, people who are so very dear to you?"

Pictures of my family and closest friends burst into my mind's eye. "Of course I do."

"How do you feel when they are near you?" pressed Manuel.

"I feel stronger, comforted, happier, more confident."

"As it should be," he replied. "You need these folks more than ever, but when you run toward them in selfishness or a desire to control or manipulate, you push them away."

I wasn't certain what Manuel was saying, but neither was I in a frame of mind to try very hard to understand.

I thought about Lynn and the cold shoulder I'd given her after my first surgery. She hadn't cared enough to be there in the waiting room while I went under the knife. Was her daughter's piano recital really more important than her brother's high-risk surgery?

And then there was Ted. I had asked him to stop by every day with one of his famous jokes to brighten my day. For the first week he had done so, but then life started to get in the way. He finally had to let me know that he still had a family and a job to tend to, and would every few days be okay? My self-centered, myopic reply surprised even me: "Your best friend only dies once."

My friend Carlos had come to the hospital every other day at first, even though it was awkward for him. He never seemed to know what to say, yet I liked just having him in the room. He didn't need to say a word. But I never told him that. I never expressed my feelings. He stopped showing up.

I reasoned that I was the one in pain. I was the one confined to a small room on the sixth floor. I was the person in danger of death. Where was their empathy? I needed them to be there. Couldn't they sacrifice a little more?

I looked at the rabbits who gazed at me from a distance. I shouted angrily at them, "Go do your own thing. Don't worry about me. I can do this without you. Forget it. I don't care!"

The rabbit with a face like my mother's ignored my shouts and hopped closer. The look in her beautiful eyes shut me up in shame.

Mom was in her eighties and was the kindest woman in the world. My suffering was breaking her aged heart. No mother should have to watch her child die, especially after having already buried her husband. I had been her care-giver. Now what would happen? She didn't deserve my bad attitude.

My self-absorbed angst began to cool, like someone had thrown ice cubes in a pan of boiling water that was no longer on the stove. The heat dissipated quickly.

Manuel gently asked, "Are you ready to try it my way?"

I was too embarrassed to look at him, but I replied, "Sorry. Yes, tell me how it's supposed to be done."

"Your backpack may hold something that will help draw the rabbits to you."

I stuck my hand into the mysterious backpack, curious what new wonder I might discover there. I would never have guessed a basin, a towel, and a large water bottle, but there they were. I stared at them in puzzlement, then turned to Manuel and shrugged.

He hinted, "Our own suffering doesn't negate the need to serve those dear to us. The Great One reached through his suffering to care for his loved ones."

I thought to myself, *I have been conveying my need much more than my love. How could I demonstrate my love more than my need?* Like a slowly rising sun, it dawned on me: while the field was indeed beautiful, there was no water to be seen. Perhaps the rabbits were thirsty.

I wrapped the towel around my waist and knelt in the grass. Then I took the water bottle and carefully began to fill the basin.

I thought about calling the rabbits to come to me, but instead I began to pronounce words of blessing. "Each of you is special and unique. Your caring glances have reassured me. I am blessed to even be near you. I want to bless you with the little I have. Is anyone thirsty?"

Almost all of the rabbits had moved within a few feet of me by the time I finished filling the basin. They were even more striking at such a close distance. Their friendly, familiar features and tender eyes radiated compassion in my direction.

I sat down on the grass beside the basin. Within a few moments, the rabbits were lapping the water as if they had not had a drink in days. Once their thirst had been satisfied, they began to surround me. Two of them hopped into my lap. Gently, I stroked the fur of the first one, and then another and another. They had no fear; in fact, quite the opposite:

each one came as close to me as it could. They were so soft and their eyes were deep pools of concern. Each one licked my hand, and if you have never been licked by a rabbit's tongue, I am sorry indeed. There are few things that feel so affectionate and happy.

As the rabbits crowded around me, one particularly rambunctious white and black rabbit fell into the water basin. He hopped out immediately, but was dripping wet. I chuckled at his damp and surprised face. I grabbed the towel from my waist and spent the next couple of minutes drying the clumsy rabbit with gentle strokes.

I felt comforted and warmed by their attention, and I gave loving attention to each one in turn. Taking my time, I petted them all and complimented each of them in some special manner.

Manuel watched the scene with joy, then offered this: "To think of the needs of others at the hour of our greatest need releases a blessing that can be gained no other way. To communicate our unspoken feelings and unstated thoughts in clear words is a great gift to those closest to us. It truly is water to their souls."

After some time, Manuel cleared his throat. I pretended not to hear. He waited a few more minutes and then said firmly, "Morty, we need to move on now."

I reluctantly stood to my feet and emptied the rest of the water into the basin. Then I spoke as clearly as possible to the rabbits crowded at my feet. "I've done all I can. Take care of each other when I am gone, okay? Stick together and be careful. I love you all!"

I watched as the rabbits moved together toward the woods from whence they had come. The fact that they were moving together brought a smile to my face. Somehow, even without me, they would be fine.

But just then, I noticed one rabbit who had left the group and headed a different direction. Manuel saw it too and concern clouded his face. He shouted a warning to the errant bunny. But it only ran faster in the wrong direction.

From nowhere, a shrill *kee-eeee-arh* pierced the air and a blur of beaks and talons knifed toward the unsuspecting hare. Manuel sprinted, waving his stick, in a desperate attempt at rescue, but the rabbit had strayed too far.

The rabbit's high squeal echoed through the meadow as a Hater Hawk's talons snatched my furry friend, carrying it away with a flap of its dark wings. Rabbit squeal and Hawk screech mingled and then faded.

I was frozen in place, shaken to the core. The love and beauty of one moment had been shattered by violence and hate and destruction. I gazed at the other rabbits disappearing together into the relative safety of the surrounding woods. *Why had the one rabbit struck out on its own in such a dangerous direction?*

Manuel also stood transfixed, and for the second time I saw tears course freely down his cheeks. He was softly repeating, "Pride kills, grace heals.

Pride kills, grace heals." I was too gripped by my own sense of horror to ask what this could mean.

Time seemed to stand still. Manuel walked over to me a few moments later. "It breaks my heart that I couldn't save all my friends. You can't either, Morty. But we dare not love less." After a long pause, he made clear that we must move on.

I picked up my crimson backpack and turned to face the rest of the valley with Manuel at my side. After a long walk in stillness, my grief was overtaken by gratitude for this wise and strong friend who walked with me. With Manuel near, I felt comforted, safe, and courageous. Deciding to apply the lesson I had learned in the meadow, I told him exactly how I felt about him. Manuel stopped, gave me one of his bear hugs, and said a simple "thank you."

We forged ahead together. The "together" part was more important to me than ever before.

Stage 4

Confusion Cave

"Why have you forsaken me?"

Presently we came to a ridge that bisected the entire valley into halves. The fifty-foot-high ridge stretched across the valley's entire width and was impassable. Its walls were like cliffs, much too steep to climb up and over. When I saw it, my heart sank. *Is this the end of our journey, even though we haven't made it through the valley?* We had already come so far; it seemed such a waste if it ended here.

Manuel, as always, seemed unconcerned. He sat himself down on a rock as I scouted for a way over the ridge. After searching to no avail, I sat down beside him. He looked me squarely in the eyes and asked, "Do you trust me?"

I answered, "I have followed you this far, haven't I?"

He replied, "But do you really trust me?"

I paused and thought about the question. Trustworthiness was a trait I highly valued. I had a reputation at work for being trustworthy. I was the honest guy, the loyal-at-all-costs guy, the promise-keeping guy.

Perhaps trustworthiness was such a big deal to me because I had grown up with such bad examples of it. Dad had walked out on Mom and us kids when I was only seven. His vow of "until death do us part" had actually meant "until a new, younger woman does us part."

My older brother had said I could trust him with my secret about liking the cutest and coolest girl in our middle school. The next morning, I sat in mind-numbing shame as the news was broadcast to the entire school over the intercom during our morning announcements. How could my own brother do this to me?

The pastor of our church was considered the most trustworthy person in our town, that is, until he was caught embezzling money from the offerings for his hidden gambling addiction.

My best friend in college was, according to him, helping my girlfriend find herself. He helped her find her way into his arms instead of mine.

I trusted few people, and for good reason. But this unusual man, Manuel, had served loyally as a guide, friend, teacher, and helper. So, when he asked me a third time, "How about it, Morty? Do you trust me?" I answered, "Well, despite the short time we've known each other, you have proven yourself trustworthy. So yes, Manuel . . . I really do trust you."

He replied, "Then I know how to proceed on our journey."

He bounced up from the rock and walked toward the ridge face, then pushed some tall shrubs aside to reveal the man-size opening of a cave. He turned and said, "Follow me."

I walked reluctantly into that cave. I hated dark, tight places. Mild claustrophobia had plagued me since I was a teen. I despised spiders and rats. Spelunking sounded to me like torture, not recreation. Indiana Jones could have his archeological adventures; I was not interested.

Nevertheless, I followed. Did I have a choice? After all, my guide was Manuel and I had just assured him that I really trusted him.

The dim light that filtered into the cave opening gave just enough illumination that I could see the large cavern that lay beyond the narrow entrance. I breathed a little easier, but stayed close to Manuel. The meager light grew ever more faint the deeper into the cave we walked. Soon I could barely make out Manuel's dark shape in front of me.

I complained to myself, *It was bad enough to make this journey under the shadow of a cloud, but now this. What I wouldn't give for a light!*

I stepped forward hesitantly and realized that now I could not see Manuel at all. I looked back toward the entrance—or toward where the entrance should have been. But I couldn't see light from any direction.

I was surrounded by darkness. Fear gripped me like a vice.

Suddenly, and strangely, I was awash in the memory of my first sleepover. I had gone with a handful of boys to my cousin's big farmhouse in the woods. Soon we had crept into the cellar and lit one lone candle. We began to tell ghost stories, each of us seeking to surpass the horror of the previous tale. Just when our terror had reached a crescendo, the candle went out, plunging us into darkness. Our young male egos were forgotten and we screamed like babies, clutching each other in fear.

I was far more terrified now.

"Manuel?" I said. No answer.

I stepped forward and reached out, but all I caught was empty air.

"Manuel?" I called with more urgency. Silence.

"Manuel, I know you are there. Quit playing. Answer me right now!"

Still nothing.

"Manuel, if this is some new test or some eternal lesson, I am refusing it. I want out of here *now*! No lessons! No funny stuff! Just turn on some light!" The black emptiness only deepened.

The darkness was suffocating. It was bad enough with Manuel a few steps ahead, but it was oppressive, haunting, and disorienting now that I was completely alone.

This couldn't be happening. I was tired of this bad dream, tired of this crazy journey. I tried to remind myself that I was actually lying in a hospital bed on the sixth floor of Valley General. I slapped myself a few times, trying to awaken there. I shouted, "This is only a dream! Only a bad dream! This is not real!" But nothing happened. I was still in a cave. Still lost in darkness. Still totally and forever alone.

Denial had sometimes seemed to be my friend—for instance, when Dad left us. I kept saying to myself, "He'll be back soon. This happens to other families, but surely not to ours." After awhile I tried a different kind of denial. I whispered to myself, "It doesn't hurt that bad. Life is better this way. I am glad he's gone." But it did hurt, life was not better, and I was not glad. I needed to grieve the loss of Dad in order to heal, but my denial, my supposed "friend," betrayed me.

Now in the cave, I had to try something other than deny that I was there. I tried walking to the right. There was nothing there. I took a couple steps to the left. Nothing. I tried a few steps back. Nothing.

Then I screamed, "Manuel! You got me into this, now get me out! Say something, *anything*!" Only a suffocating silence was heard.

Now anger seized me. "Why me?" I shouted. "Why not some dope-smoking wife beater, or some homeless man with nothing left to desire but death's knock on his door? You've got the wrong guy! Why me? Answer me that, oh wise one!" Silence.

"Manuel, dammit, answer me now or else!" I didn't know what "or else" meant—I certainly wasn't in any position to mete out retribution or dictate terms. But it felt good to scream my wrath at the top of my lungs—and in language hardly typical of me. Yet the release lasted only a moment before my rage felt empty and pointless. What good was wrath going to do? Maybe I was using unnecessarily fast the little bit of oxygen in this God-forsaken place.

My mind raced to find an escape. Perhaps I could bargain with Manuel to get me out of here—if he was still there and could hear me, that is.

When I was five years old, my mother, my sister, and I had been caught in a horrific hailstorm on Route 66. The hail smashed out the windshield of our car. Trembling on the floorboard of the backseat, I had bargained with God: "If you get me out of this, I will stop sleeping with my night-light on!"

What had I been thinking? I guess I had figured that God knew how frightened I was of the darkness, so I could prove I trusted Him by throwing out my little cowboy night-light. Just then, the hail had stopped and we were spared. Each night during the following year, I regretted the bargain I had struck with God every time Mom shut out the lights!

It had worked then, so why not try it now? I thought to myself, *I will at least try to bargain with the one who maybe can't be bargained with. It may be a long shot, but it's a shot.*

"Manuel, if you will just light a match, or answer me, or do something, I promise that I will do anything you want, anything. Just get me out of here!" No answer. No deal. No Manuel.

After another several minutes of stumbling this way and that, I was getting nowhere. I sank down to the cave's dirt floor in dismal hopelessness. *It's no use. There is no point to all of this*, I thought. Depression settled over me like a smothering blanket.

I was nearly done, really done. Before that, however, I mustered what voice remained and shouted, "Manuel, Manuel, why did you forsake me? I thought we were friends! I trusted you!"

With those words, the physical darkness became a spiritual darkness that invaded my very soul. I sat in the dark and the dirt and sobbed quietly like an abandoned orphan.

Kee-eeee-arh, kee-eeee-arh!!

Terror leaped into the toxic maelstrom of emotions that already threatened to drown me. *Those awful hawks were in the cave! They must have tracked me, hunted me down in this damnable cave.* The sound of death was in their hateful screeching. I had no doubt that their beady black eyes could see clearly in this ink-well of awful darkness.

In my panic, I suddenly remembered my backpack. How could I have forgotten it? Surely the answer to this death trap was waiting there for me.

I imagined a flashlight, or even a spotlight—anything to pierce this darkness, frighten the hawks away, and lead me forward—and out!

I stuck my trembling hand in and felt around, yanking out a piece of fabric. I examined it by touch and concluded that it must be the wrapping for some kind of headlamp or spotlight. I thrust my hand into the backpack again, grasping desperately for a light of any kind . . . for anything else . . . but there was nothing else. My handful of hope burst like a balloon. The *kee-eeee-arhs* roared closer and more menacingly than before.

With one hand clutching the fabric, I wailed in abject hopelessness and fear. As I waited for razor-sharp talons to sink into my skin, I became aware of the distinctive feel of the fabric I held. Stretching it out, I could feel that it was about five feet wide and five feet long, about the size of a baby blanket. I ran my fingers across the fabric and it felt both soft and strong. Every six inches there was a seam, as if pieces of cloth had been sewn together.

I held it to my face and inhaled a delicate but delightful fragrance. It smelled like my newborn son after his first bath. I clung to the blanket, wrapping it around my shoulders and face. As I did, the screeches of the hawks grew more distant. I pulled the fabric tighter. In the cold, dark cave, it warmed my body and soul.

I inhaled the soothing scent of the blanket again and again. And as I did, I imagined my helplessness as an infant, my inability to move anywhere or communicate anything but my need. I could not care for myself in any way.

A childlike trust began to seep into my soul. I pictured my mother wrapping me tightly in my baby blanket. I felt the warmth, the security, the soothing comfort of that act of love. I could almost hear her caring voice assuring me, "It's okay, little Morty. It's going to be okay."

I thought of my baby daughter and the "Blue Blankie" she had carried everywhere, just like Linus in *Peanuts*. She couldn't sleep unless Blue Blankie was held tightly in her arms. She could be screaming her lungs out, but if I wrapped her snugly in Blue Blankie, soon she was peaceful and cooing. She trusted me and she had her Blankie.

Perhaps that was the message of this blanket: childlike trust. Trust based not on the experience of the moment but on the integrity of the caregiver. I decided that I could continue screaming in fear or I could sit peacefully in trust, praying for Manuel to return.

Making my choice, I lay down, still wrapped securely in the blanket. I stopped trying to figure everything out. I accepted that I was only a child, a child who didn't have the answers I wanted or the ability to change my mortality. I was a child in need of nurture and security, a child with a blanket given to him by someone who cared deeply about him. I pictured Manuel's kind eyes. I trusted, and I fell asleep with the warm blanket wrapped around me.

Then, I don't know how much later, I felt a strong but gentle hand shaking me awake. "Hey, Amigo. It's time to go." Manuel was there! Manuel was back. Manuel was with me. My heart leaped at the joy of his touch!

I opened my eyes and thought, *It's no longer pitch black.* There really was a dim light seeping into the darkness, opening a way ahead, a way out.

My joy at deliverance, however, was soon replaced by troubled questions. "Manuel, where were you when I needed you?" I demanded an answer, and with only a thinly veiled tone of hostility.

"Watching you," Manuel answered, without any evidence of hurt or offense at my harsh tone.

"What were you doing when I shouted my lungs out?" I asked with a little less wrath.

"Listening to your every breath," he replied with deep sincerity.

"What were you up to while I was asleep?" I quizzed as my anger ebbed.

"Digging. Changing this cave into a tunnel. Making a way through the darkness. Notice anything different since you fell asleep?"

I looked ahead at the distant light trickling into the cave. Manuel was right: This was no longer a cave. A cave is darkness that leads to a dead end. But a tunnel leads through darkness to the light.

In the soft light of the tunnel, my annoyance faded into deep gratitude for Manuel's presence and what I now realized he had been doing for us.

"Why didn't you let me know you were near or what you were up to?" I asked in a much more respectful tone.

He drew in a couple of deep breaths and let them out in what seemed like bottomless sighs. It was as if he were holding back tears. He finally replied, "Some levels of trust are only learned through silence and not knowing everything."

"What about the blanket I found in the backpack?" I queried.

"The Great One was wrapped in a blanket at birth and at death. Life is a journey from the blanket of an infant's trust to the blanket of an elderly man's trust at death. There is no other way forward through Shadow Valley," Manuel said. "Now follow me."

With that, and all that now had to be thought about, we walked onward toward the light at the end of the tunnel.

As we picked our way toward the light, I recalled the oldest woman at my church. This lady had encountered many difficult circumstances during her life's journey. Yet she was a woman of such calm conviction and simple trust. She was highly esteemed by all. She was known for simple words of counsel like, "If God brings you *to* it, He will bring you *through* it!"

I now had a new appreciation for that woman's words. By his love and effort, Manuel had broken through the cave's dead end and made a passageway that led to a new chapter of my journey.

I began to hum a melody from church, and sing the only words I could remember: *Through it all, through it all . . . I've learned to trust in God. Through it all, through it all, I've learned to depend upon His Word.* Indeed, I had!

I was still humming when we stepped out of the tunnel into a grassy meadow. I felt older and younger at the same time. I had come through something incredibly challenging, but the victory Manuel had provided had softened me into a dependent child instead of a boastful hero.

Stage 5

Satisfaction Spring

"I thirst"

Manuel and I meandered from the cave toward the end of the valley. We chatted about my life. We talked about my hobbies, my dreams, my different career positions, and my possessions. Our relationship had reached a much deeper level than before the cave.

There now was an ease to our conversation, as if we'd been friends for a lifetime. Being with Manuel felt like leaning back in my favorite recliner . . . so familiar, so restful, so restorative. He truly was my friend!

After an hour of walking, the terrain became very arid, desert-like. The temperature on the valley floor rose dramatically. I was sweating more with each passing step. I also noticed an increasing level of pain.

The dull pain, which had plagued me for the past six weeks in the "real world," seemed to have followed me to this valley. The pain was centered around my heart and felt like someone had strapped a cement block to my chest. Now, as the temperature climbed, so did my pain level. It felt like a slow-burning fire. The outer heat and the inner heat wrung every bit of moisture from my body. My tongue swelled from dehydration. My lips chapped and began to crack.

Yet, determined to keep faith with my friend, and I now was sure he really was my friend, I kept silent. I had embarrassed myself in the cave, whimpering like a child, wrapping myself in a baby blanket. I considered myself a strong man. I had been relatively successful in life. People thought of me as courageous and resourceful. So I gritted my teeth and kept marching.

I so wanted to be strong, and to prove my trust in Manuel. He had proven himself a friend who would watch out for me. He knew where we were. He could see how it was affecting me. He surely knew what to do. I believed, although I struggled with a little unbelief. After all, it was still me.

To deal with my suffering, I began to take my mind elsewhere. I focused on the reflection of Paradise I had seen back in the pond. Manuel had advised me to remember that vision and use it, and so I did now. The promise of Paradise gave me hope that this difficult journey was headed somewhere wonderful. I might be on a hard way, but it was a holy way.

Envision it. Anticipate it. Meditate on it. This process, hopefully not just a mind game, gave me strength and courage to press on. Without that vivid picture, that vision of Paradise, my suffering would have seemed pointless, and probably intolerable. Without that promise, the journey thus far would have been nothing but a cruel joke. No wonder Manuel had been so adamant about burning the Paradise image into my mind.

On and on we trudged through the sand, straight ahead, one step by another step, followed by one more painful, burning step. Eventually, thoughts of Paradise faded. I prayed hard. I sought to trust deeply. Nothing helped. I was so thirsty!

I recalled my grandfather slowly dying. He was in and out of consciousness. His lips became so dry that every few minutes I took a small, moist, glycerin swab and wet his lips and mouth. On the rare occasion when he was half conscious, he called for water. I craved just one of those swabs for my own mouth now.

I thought, *This is what it must feel like to die.* I could keep silent no longer, and through cracked lips I tried to speak. But my tongue had become stuck to the roof of my mouth. With great effort, I loosened it and tried once more.

"I am so thirsty!" I slurred with an agony that surprised even me. I had caught the attention of my "friend."

Manuel stopped and, with a compassionate gaze, said, "I know, but I was waiting for you to tell me. Sharing your needs is not weakness, Morty, it's wisdom."

Then he pointed to a nearby hill. Atop the small incline were three trees and a strange car-sized rock. "Head for the rock," Manuel directed. I had been looking in that direction before, but had not seen the hill or the rock. After rubbing my eyes, I was convinced it was no mirage.

With new hope, I willed myself forward until we arrived at the base of the hill. Although it was only a short climb, I thought there was no way I could make it to the top. But I had to try. Slowly, step by agonizing step, I ascended. I stumbled several times. The weight of my backpack, which had been unnoticeable before, now felt like the weight of the whole world. I took off the pack and Manuel picked it up and carried it for me as we continued up the hill.

After what seemed an eternity, I reached the rock and fell beside it. The pain, the thirst, the exhaustion, all piled on top of me. I wanted to die—not later, not soon, not eventually, but *right now*. I lay there and silently prayed that it would happen. When finally I admitted I couldn't wish my end into existence, I focused on my thirst once more.

I remembered all the great drinks I had tasted during my life: fizzy sodas, delicious juices, cool teas, refreshing lemonades. With each new memory, a shiver of pleasure ran through my body. But soon my mouth and mind felt drier and less satisfied than ever. The memories were enjoyable, but none could satisfy my present thirst. I needed water, real water, and lots of it.

"I don't see any water. Where's the water?" I pleaded, looking blankly at Manuel.

"In the rock," Manuel replied, "in the rock."

"What do you mean?"

Manuel smiled gently. "There is a spring in the middle of the rock."

"How do we get the water out of the spring?"

"Now, that is the big problem," said Manuel.

I pulled myself on top of the flat rock. In the middle was a three-foot-wide hole. I looked down. Sure enough, I could see running water. There was a spring in the rock! I guessed that it was about six feet below the rock's surface. I could smell the water, hear the water, see the water— but smelling, hearing, and seeing only made the agony of my thirst deeper. I slumped to the ground in despair.

There was no way that I could reach the water. I was stuck, nailed to the reality of my weakness and nearby death, with salvation so close by! Then Manuel's words broke into my consciousness. "You must focus on what you still have, not on what you have lost."

What craziness is that? What do I still have? What help can I take advantage of? What can I use to bring me relief and comfort? Isn't all lost, gone?

Maybe not. When I was willing to look on the positive side, I saw that I did have two things still left, my backpack and my friend.

Manuel had laid my backpack against the rock. I struggled to it and reached my hand to the bottom. I had learned by now to not even guess what might be waiting there. A bucket with a rope would have been nice, but no. Instead, I found an extremely large and completely dry sponge.

This might work, I thought, *but only with some help*. I turned to my friend.

"Manuel, could you help me quench my thirst?" I offered the sponge to him.

"I thought you would never ask, Morty. I would be delighted to help."

Manuel took the sponge and strode toward the middle tree on the hilltop. He broke off a slender, six-foot-long branch. With one swift motion, he threaded the sponge through the branch, making sure it was secure. Then he leaped on top of the rock and immersed the sponge deep into the water, letting it linger for just a moment. The sponge oozed and dripped water as Manuel stepped down to where I lay in torment on the ground.

Carefully, Manuel brought the sponge to my parched lips and swabbed them. I opened my mouth and the water gently slid in—not too little, not too much. Rivulets of water opened a larger and larger channel in my scorched throat, and tiny swallows gave way to life-giving gulps.

It was the purest, most blessed drink I had ever experienced. It tasted like Paradise in liquid form. This had to be the beverage of heaven. It was so refreshing, so life-imparting, so nourishing. No other liquid had ever satisfied my craving like that fresh spring water.

Time and time again, Manuel brought the dripping sponge to my mouth, and then he squeezed it over my face, head, neck, and body. Life rushed into my veins. I could feel the liquid in every cell of my body. I was saturated from head to toe.

I thought back to one blazing summer day of my childhood. Our small un-air-conditioned house was like a furnace, so Mom loaded us up in the station wagon and drove us to the plaza at City Hall. In front of the courthouse was a large fountain with water cascading off its twenty-foot-high bowl. On many previous summer afternoons we had begged to jump into the fountain. Each time we were met with Mom's sternest gaze, "It's not allowed!"

That was then, but somehow this day was different. We were shocked when Mom said, "Okay kids, jump in!" We spent the next two hours splashing in the cool water, laughing, and playing. Mom even waded with us. The policeman, who usually strictly enforced the "no wading" rule, started a splashing war with us. It was unbelievable!

That day was a highlight of my difficult childhood. Today, at this rock, it was like that again, but much, much more.

As Manuel drenched me once again, I realized that this was no ordinary water. My thirst was being quenched not just at a physical level but at emotional and spiritual levels as well. The inner anguish I had been battling since my journey began gave way to sweet peace. My anger was washed away. Even my self-pity was rinsed off and replaced with gratitude. It was altogether marvelous, beyond explanation, beyond expectation.

As I leaned against the rock, dripping from head to toe, I reminisced about my baptism in my early twenties. Pastor Kern had been deadly serious in our preparatory class. Every word was spoken slowly and with a gravity that made me reconsider my readiness and desire for baptism—so much so that I voiced my hesitancy to him.

That wise minister had put his old arm around me, looked me in the eyes, and said, "It's like marriage, Morty. No one who makes that vow fully understands what it means to pledge a lifetime to another person. No one who says 'I do' is entirely prepared for or even aware of the journey they on which they are embarking. But they trust their heart and the heart of their partner. Baptism is like that, son. If you mean it as much as you can mean it right now, and if you trust the God you commit yourself to, then the waters of baptism will launch you into a new life beyond what you could imagine. Go for it, son. It will grow on you!"

On that baptism day, when I came up from the water and stood drenched, the church folk had applauded. Pastor Kern high-fived me. Mom beamed. I felt like a fifty-pound weight sitting on my heart had instantly dissolved in the water. My whole being was a big grin. I had begun a big journey, a really good one. It might be a hard way at times, but it would always be a holy way if I would just keep going.

That was then. And now—so much later, so much farther down the road?

I was experiencing that same radiant satisfaction. Death was still on the horizon, but even it could not threaten my contentedness. The physical pain was now only a whisper in my chest. I was energized and determined to reach the end of Shadow Valley!

When Manuel and I were both thoroughly soaked, we leaned against the rock and the warm sun kissed us with joy. The temperature had dropped twenty degrees, and it was perfect. We kept chuckling like two schoolboys who had just heard the bell announcing summer break. I was free and giddy. My good, good friend was close to my side. More music came into my head.

I launched into an old camp song I had learned somewhere. I botched the verses but aced the chorus: "Spring up, oh well, within my soul and make me whole." Manuel added a few "splish-splashes" at just the right places, and applauded wildly at the end of our very armature but very joyous rendition.

At that very second I heard a very faint *kee-eeee-arh* from the distant sky, but barely a twinge of fear fluttered across my heart. It was hard to be scared when seated next to Manuel. Suddenly, some goopy white matter fell from the sky and onto my head. I turned to Manuel, "Is that what I think it is?"

He barely suppressed a laugh and said, "They hate it when my friends are happy! Always looking for a way to rain on the parade!" We both started laughing.

He squeezed more water from the sponge and washed all the filth away, and we kept laughing through the grossness of it all. When I was cleaned up, we resumed our celebration right where we had left off, refusing to let anything steal the joy of the moment. The faint *kee-eeee-arh* was entirely gone.

After another song, we sat quietly, slowly drying in the gentle sun. Then I said, "I feel like there were some important lessons I was to learn through all of this. You want to help a friend out here?"

Manuel, ever the teacher, was quick to respond. As he often did, he used questions to guide my exploration. "Did you find that your physical thirst was quenched by your prayers?"

"No," I answered, "they strengthened me, but I still needed water. My body and spirit seem connected but not synonymous. I was a complete, disconnected mess."

He smiled widely. "*Bueno!* Good job! As long you are on this side of death, you must address your physical needs with the right form of care until it's clear nothing can cure you any longer."

Then he probed further, "And was it wise to just assume that I knew what you needed?"

I thought and then acknowledged, "No. You probably knew all along, but I needed to state my desires and needs so that you could respond to them effectively."

"Right, Morty, right. People want to know how they can comfort you on your journey, but often they don't have any idea. They don't want to do the wrong thing so they feel insecure around you. Unambiguously communicating what you need or want helps others know what they can do for you."

I sure knew that people back in that hospital room were uncomfortable around me. They were not sure what to say or do, nor was I. This was a strange new journey with few signposts along the way for any of us.

Then Manuel asked, "And could you get this water on your own?"

"No. I needed help from someone who could bring the water to me. I needed you."

"It is good to be strong, Morty, but not to be independent. People belong together, loving and sharing and serving. It is better to give than to receive, but to receive is also very good. The Great One twice asked for help when he was thirsty, once at a well and once on a hill."

His next question surprised me. It was an easy one to answer. "Morty, what did you think of the water you just drank?"

"It was infinitely more satisfying than the finest drink I have ever tasted. It quenched not only the thirst of my tongue but of my heart as well!" He smiled.

My mind flashed back to all the things I had pursued for satisfaction in life. Growing up, I knew my heart was thirsty for something, and though I half-heartedly believed in God, he hadn't quenched my thirst. I had chased my athletic dreams as if being "all-state" would fulfill me. Then it was the homecoming queen and sexual conquests. I graduated to desiring the big job, the new car, the nice house, the yearly cruise. Those all quieted my hungry heart, but only for a little while. Even my noble pursuits of volunteering at the Boys Club and helping at the soup kitchen couldn't satisfy my deepest thirst.

But now, finally, I had found the perfect drink. This water from the rock was the elixir of life that I had been searching for. I was fully satisfied.

"And that, my friend, is why this place is called Satisfaction Spring," Manuel announced. I could only smile in complete agreement.

He continued, "This water runs like rivers in Paradise. There, you don't just sip it from time to time. There it is served with every meal. You wash your face in it, you bathe in it, swim in it, and dance in it. You are going to love it, Morty!"

I really believed him. And, for the first time since my death sentence was pronounced by that doctor, I was looking forward more than backward. It was a hard, but holy way leading to a wonderfully holy conclusion.

After we were fully dry and completely rested, Manuel popped an unexpected question. "Hey, are you hungry, Morty?"

I had not realized it until that moment. "Actually, I'm starving. But I don't see any fast food places close by."

Manuel snickered at my lame attempt at humor. "Well, how about your backpack? Maybe someone packed you a lunch."

I grabbed my backpack, hoping I would reach in and find steak and lobster. But inside the backpack was nothing but a red-and-white checked tablecloth. I pulled it out and quipped, "I don't eat these without cooking them." More lame humor.

Manuel gave me a courtesy laugh, then directed me to spread the cloth across one end of the rock. I did as he said and discovered that it fit perfectly. While I smoothed the tablecloth, Manuel reached into his own backpack. By the time I turned around, he was holding a huge loaf of freshly baked bread. You could see the steam rising from it. The aroma was heavenly. He put it down on the tablecloth and then reached again into his pack, pulling out a bottle of red wine and one large crystal goblet.

I was not much of a drinker, having a glass of wine only on very special occasions. But I had been a waiter in a high-priced Italian restaurant during college and I knew fine wines when I saw them. This was easily a $2,000 bottle of wine. The whole time I waited tables, I had sold only one bottle of this quality.

Manuel opened the bottle and, with one flowing motion, poured the goblet fuller and fuller, to the brim, and kept pouring until it overflowed. I watched in amazement. The aroma of the wine and bread together was beyond imagination. Manuel asked, "Shall we give thanks?" Before I could respond, he looked to the sky and with humble confidence said, "Thank you, Father, for the bread and wine which satisfies our souls. May it nourish us now and forever. Amen!"

He broke the bread, handed me one portion, and took a huge bite from the other half. Even before he finished chewing, he took a long gulp of wine.

I followed his example. The bread tasted divine, so earthy and bursting with flavor. I took a sip of the wine and its flavor whirled across my taste buds with the grace and beauty of a ballerina. I took another mouthful. It was like a party in my mouth.

As the meal continued, Manuel asked me to share stories from my life. So I flipped back through the pages of my past and told him about the good times and bad times, like good friends would do with each other. We continued to eat, and smiled and groaned together as we savored every bite and sip, and as we shared my stories.

I couldn't escape comparing this meal to my first communion after my baptism. I had come straight to church from an early morning football practice and was famished. Pastor Kern broke off a quarter-sized piece of stale bread and handed me a half-swallow sized cup of cheap juice. As I took them, he smiled as if he had done me a huge favor. I remembered wondering if God or the church was too broke to serve better food and bigger portions. What Manuel was serving was more like it. This was the real deal!

It had always struck me as odd that something so physical, so earthy, as bread and wine could impart something so spiritual to my life. Pastor Kern had talked about communion being the intersection of earth and heaven, the place where our faith transformed an historical event into a spiritual reality for today. I now understood his words much more clearly as Manuel and I dined.

The bread of this meal was more than flour and water; it was life. As I ate the broken bread, my hunger was sated and my hurts were healed. As I drank the wine, I forgot all my failures, which had been playing like a broken record in my mind. It was like someone just turned off the screaming stereo and threw away the old record. Sharing that meal with Manuel also brought us closer together than we had been before. I felt one with him more than with anyone in my entire life, even my mother and wife. This was true *communion*.

We ate and drank, he and I together, until we were both full. The meal was simple, yet it was the finest of my life. It was life!

After eating, we lay down in the grass and were soon napping in the sun. I woke a short time later to find Manuel sitting on the rock whittling some kind of flute. He tried it out and it produced a high, clear, pleasant tone. It was soon obvious that he was a musical expert; the flute burst forth in sweet melody. It was incredible music. I wanted him never to quit playing. They were the holy notes of life itself, eternal life being played especially for me.

But after a few minutes, Manuel stopped and said, "Morty, we are nearing the end of the valley. It's time to move on. Ready?"

I really wasn't. I didn't want to go. This hilltop had brought me such joy, healing, satisfaction, and life. "Can't we stay here forever?" I pleaded.

He replied, "Morty, have you ever ridden a bus to the airport? The bus is so far superior to walking all the way there. You are so glad that you boarded and so thankful for the air-conditioning and the soft seats. But you know that the bus will never take you across the ocean. It's only meant to transport you to the airport. That's where you will really take off. That's what this hill is like. It's a launching pad, not the destination, the beginning, a really good beginning, but not the end."

That made sense to me, although I didn't really like his answer. But I knew that my friend was wise, even all wise, so I happily went with him. We walked down the hill. It was time to press forward, to explore the next adventure between here and the end of the valley.

Stage 6

Legacy Lane

"It is finished!"

I had new strength and walked with more spring in my step—after all, I had been to the spring of life! But it wasn't long until the pain returned, not as intense as before, but more pervasive. The dull ache spread through my chest and torso and then down to my legs. I sensed that Manuel and I were drawing nearer to the end of our journey. My pain told me, and when I looked toward the end of Shadow Valley, my vision confirmed it. The valley was narrowing. At the furthest point, which had finally come into view, the walls looked as if they actually came almost together.

We traveled on, and arid sands gave way to rolling pastures. My mind flashed back to scenes of my favorite childhood movie, *The Wizard of Oz*. I recalled the Scarecrow's need for a brain, the Lion's need for courage, and

the Tin Man's need for a heart. On their journey they discover something really surprising. What they need is already theirs!

The Scarecrow says, "Success, fame, and fortune, they're all illusions. All there is that is real is the friendship that two can share." My friendship with Manuel seemed to me now as if it were the only real thing, the only necessary thing.

The cowardly Lion asks, "What makes a king out of a slave?" His answer is "Courage." On this journey through Shadow Valley, I had been both a slave to fear and increasingly a courageous king. Now I refused to be a slave any longer. I may have moments of fear, but they would no longer master me. Manuel's presence filled me with a solid courage.

The Wizard counsels the Tin Man about the advantages of being heartless: "As for you, my galvanized friend, you want a heart. You don't know how lucky you are not to have one. Hearts will never be practical until they can be made unbreakable."

While that makes good sense, in a way, I always loved the Tin Man's reply: "But I still want one." Having no heart would certainly have made living, and especially dying, much easier in some ways. But the joy of love is only as great as the heart's willingness to be broken.

At the thought of now leaving my dear ones, my heart *was* breaking. But I still cherished the privilege of having a heart, of having loved and been loved. It filled me with a deeper joy than I thought possible.

How such ache and awe could co-exist inside one chest was beyond my imagination. But it did!

And I thought about Dorothy, the little girl lost in Oz. All she wants is to go home. I truly wanted to go home, back to the hospital, back to my house—but now I was less sure where my real home was. I had lived in the same place for three decades and had never before been unsure about where to find home. But a new vision of home was forming in my heart.

What had been home for my short years on earth was really more like a nice hotel—very pleasant and comfortable, a place to unpack my bags, but not always a place to remain. My earth place had been somewhere to grow older--but not to settle into forever. It was a rest area on my journey, but not my destination.

I was beginning to understand that my *real* home was "somewhere over the rainbow," a place where "dreams you dare to dream really do come true," a place where "troubles melt like lemon drops." Home was somewhere beyond Shadow Valley, a place where skies are perpetually blue. I had seen glimpses of it at Paradise Pond, and consumed a little of it at Satisfaction Spring, and now my heart was torn between a desire to visit earth a little longer and a desire to go to my final and true home. I agreed with Dorothy: "There is no place like home."

Consumed by my thoughts, I did not realize that we had come to a lane edged by oak trees. As I became aware of our new surroundings, I saw that it was a narrow lane, not more than fifty feet wide.

On each side stretched a lengthy row of oak trees. It was quite the elegant approach to something important.

The trees on opposite sides of the lane could not have been more different from each other. The oaks on the right side of the lane were filled with life. Vibrant green leaves crowded thick, healthy branches. Acorns hung in abundant clusters. These oaks were spectacular, and my eyes were riveted to these glorious trees.

I couldn't help but notice, however, that the oaks on the left side of the lane were bare, with no leaves and no acorns. Their twisted branches were like dried-out skeletons reaching to the gloomy sky. It was a haunting and depressing view.

Kee-eeee-arh, kee-eeee-arh! The sinister screeches startled me. I cast my gaze to the sky, searching for the vile birds as I grabbed for Manuel's arm. The sky was empty—but then I saw them. The Hater Hawks were roosting in the trees on the left side of the lane. They had made their nests in the naked branches and, thankfully, seemed uninterested in our presence for now.

When I found the courage to speak, I asked Manuel about the difference between the trees on opposite sides of the lane. He got one of those distant looks in his eyes, a look that mixed sadness and glory. Finally, he replied, "After a tree dies, some of them come back alive to a lavish existence. Others, tragically, refuse this life. Their existence is more like an ongoing death."

He paused and brushed a tear from the corner of his eye, groaning heavily. He gathered himself and continued in a tone of animated enthusiasm. "Those who regain life have life far more abundant than they had before death. They are vibrant with life, always productive, always green, with sap pulsing through their branches. The Great One said, 'If a person believes, he shall live, even though he dies.'"

I didn't really understand, but I continued gazing down the lane and then noticed something I had failed to see at first. In front of each oak, on both sides of the lane, was a small grey tombstone. Each tombstone was exactly the same size and shape. They stretched as far as I could see.

I looked more closely. Each tombstone bore a similar inscription. In large letters was the full name of a person. Under the name appeared "Arrival Date" and "Departure Date," with days, months, and years carefully identified and carved into the stone.

Manuel and I walked down the lane slowly, and I looked at many of the individual oaks. There were strange carvings on each and every tree. Some were completely covered in carvings. Others had far fewer markings. I wanted to look at the carvings more closely, but I was hesitant to walk past the tombstones to the trees. I looked at Manuel, who gave me a nod as if to say, "Go on, take a good look."

I walked up to a medium-sized tree and studied the curious carvings. I discovered that they were short phrases about the life of a person. Insight slowly dawned on me. I realized there was a connection between the name on the tombstone and the tree. It was as if each oak was a "Life Tree" of the person named on the nearby tombstone.

I remembered once walking through cemeteries with friends when I was younger, looking at tombstones and wondering about the persons buried below. We would occasionally make up stories about "Bill Bokins" and his 69-year-long life as we lounged atop his final resting place. These impromptu story-telling times always ended in raucous laughter.

But there was no light-heartedness in this moment. True-life stories were staring me in the face. These carvings were serious and somehow sacred.

As I studied the carvings carefully, I realized that the person's youngest days were at the top of the trunk and the last days were carved along the bottom. There were two curious shapes in the middle. One was a perfect heart and the other a rectangular box. They were deeply grooved into the tree and larger than any of the other carvings.

I began to read aloud some of the phrases from different trees: "Started a new job at bank." "Married Jeannie Brown." Some seemed quite significant: "Had a baby boy named Joey." Others seemed trivial: "Visited Mary in the hospital." Some were events: "Won homecoming king." Others were facts about likes and dislikes: "Hated church services." "Liked baseball." Others were beliefs: "Believed in fate." "Believed in reincarnation." I was most surprised to find a few sins of the person listed on the tree: "Slept with Ann." "Cheated on tax return." "Habitual gossiper." Each Life Tree told it like it was.

The carvings called up a memory I had stored away from my own adolescent years. Tawni and I had stood beside a large oak tree far off the beaten path. With my handy Swiss Army knife we had whittled, "Tawni + Morty = Love Forever." One of my most regretted sins took place under that tree. The relationship was over in a year long, but the carving remained there to this day.

I studied one tree and then another. After only a few minutes of reading Life Tree messages of this life and that life, I felt like I had a basic understanding of who these people had really been. I was fascinated by the legacy each had left.

I was most curious about the heart space and the box space in the middle of each tree. I finally had to ask, "Manuel, what do these spaces mean?"

Manuel replied with a question, as he often did: "By reading what's in them, what do you think?"

I walked to a few more trees and contemplated what was written there.

In each heart were six words, never more and never less. "Lived for the next good time." "Was admired as a real success." "Worked hard, played hard, got rich." "Pursued inner peace and harmonious living." "Loved his work, family, and golf." They seemed to be summary statements of the Life Tree, a central truth for understanding the person.

In each box were statements of varying lengths that recounted the person's cause of death. "Cancer." "Murdered." "Motorcycle accident."

"Heart attack." "AIDS." In the vast majority of the boxes, however, there was an additional statement which seemed to indicate the attitude in which the person had faced death.

I was struck by a thought I had never considered before. Only a small percentage of people die suddenly. Most die gradually. As they age, or as their disease progresses, or as the warning signs grow more alarming, they realize that they are coming to death's door. People deny it, ignore it, hope it will go away, or try to take an alternative route. But, ultimately, one by one, all people die.

It occurred to me now that people have a choice about how they face death, how they exit, how they live their last days or weeks or months. While disease and age can weaken the body and mind, it does not have to destroy the will. The power to choose is usually present in some form until the last breath.

"Feared and closed down." "Trusted in their optimism." "Was angry and bitter." "Wallowed in self-pity." "Became very religious." "Stared into space with an empty mind." "Joked about it until the last hour." No two phrases were the same.

I was quiet as I reflected on how many different ways there are to face death. I had done enough historical reading to realize that last words may or may not be important. But it appeared that last attitudes are always significant.

Manuel cleared his throat and said, "Morty, we better move on down the lane." I rejoined him and we slowly walked on.

After about a mile, there was a gap in the trees, a football-field length of nothing but green grass. Then the oak trees began again, but they were quite different now. On each side of the road stood quite common-looking oaks. There was no obvious difference between the trees on the left and the right, and I noticed with great relief that there were no Hater Hawks at roost. Looking closer, I could see that similar carvings as before covered the trees on both sides. The same grey tombstones stood like sentinels in front of each one.

Instead of asking Manuel about the difference between these and the previous trees, I decided just to keep walking and observing. I paused at one of the grey tombstones and immediately noticed the difference: *There was no Departure Date.*

Like a child who has solved a riddle, I proudly exclaimed, "These trees haven't died yet!"

"Correct . . . not yet," was Manuel's reply.

We continued our walk down the lane. The farther we walked, the more the leaves on the oak trees changed, as if we had started in spring and were moving toward winter. The color of the leaves gradually changed. Then leaves began to fall to the ground—at first a few, then many, then most.

Manuel had been picking up his pace, but he stopped suddenly. I thought perhaps we were almost to the end of the oaks, but then I glanced to the side of the lane. The sight jolted me as if I had grabbed an electric wire. I literally fell to my knees in shock. In large and ornate letters on a gray granite tombstone was *my name* and my date of birth! Standing behind was a medium oak tree. It was my Life Tree! Only a few leaves remained on its branches; the rest had fallen to the ground and lay inches deep around the trunk.

The fast-approaching finality of my life hit me like never before. Looking further down the lane, I could actually see the end of Shadow Valley just ahead.

"It's almost finished!" I said. Manuel only smiled.

After recovering from my initial distress, I began to feel a rising sense of curiosity. I wondered, *What does my tree have carved on it?* I got up, stepped past the tombstone and up to my Life Tree. I began to read from as high as I could, phrases that described my college days. Childhood and middle school were higher and beyond my view. "Helped in special education class." "Went to church occasionally." "Was into *The Grateful Dead*" (how ironic that was in this moment). "Had sex with Tawni." I blushed and glanced to see if Manuel saw what I was reading.

There were several inscriptions I longed to wish away, but they were indelibly marked. As I bemoaned some of the marks, my friend spoke with compassion, "Don't worry about the bad ones. Insurance covered those."

"I don't get it," I replied.

Manuel had a twinkle in his eye. "You had some accidents due to poor driving, but you were covered. You don't have to pay for those. It's all about who your insurance provider is," he said with a grin. I still didn't follow.

He pointed to a carving I hadn't seen. In large letters were the words, "Trusted the Great One."

I knew the date. That had been quite a night. My college roommate had challenged me to consider the reality of my faith. I was a pretty good guy. Sure, I partied too hard sometimes and lived for myself almost all the time. But I also went to church occasionally and did some volunteering. My roommate took out his worn Bible and asked, "Do you think this Book should have the last word about what you believe?"

"I guess so," I replied.

Over the next couple of hours, I felt my heart peeled open, layer after layer, by the wisdom he shared. The words got to my inner core. I became convinced that life is absolutely meaningless if this life is all there is. And if what my roommate showed me was true, it changed everything. There was hope, life made sense, and if I chose this path I really couldn't lose. It would make the life I was living mean something and give me the best shot at life after this life. I had made a big decision and trusted the hero of the Book.

As I looked now at my Life Tree, I noticed that the carvings began to change after that. "Worshipped authentically." "Gave generously." "Volunteered at homeless shelter." "Prayed diligently for his son, Sam." Oh, there were still some I wished I could erase. "Impatient with wife." "Swore at bad drivers." "Wasted time on too much TV." But still, it was obvious that I had been truly changed that night.

I stopped reading when my eyes fell on the deeply engraved heart and box. Both were empty. The wood within the outlines lay smooth, waiting for a carving. I had a longing just then to complete my tree, to bring my story to a conclusion, a good conclusion. I yearned to mark the heart of my tree with six words of noble summary. I desired to die well, to fill in the box with significant words by deliberately and carefully choosing my approach to death.

A panicked thought gripped my heart. *What if I'm too late?* After all, it appeared my death was just ahead, a few more steps down the lane.

Manuel answered my unasked question. "It's never too late to choose how it ends until it has ended. At any moment, a person can decide, *This is not how my story is going to end*!"

Inspired by his words and the passion in my heart, I began to scan for something with which I could to carve. But all I found at the base of the tree were fallen leaves and small flowers. I grew disheartened, wondering how I would complete my tree without a knife. Then I recalled my crimson backpack. Surely it had one more item in its mysterious depths.

I removed the backpack, threw open the flap, and reached my hand down, feeling for a knife or large carving tool. But I found nothing. Perhaps this time I was mistaken, or maybe there was another clue I had missed about where to find a carving tool.

In a last desperate effort, I reached deep in the pack and my fingers found a tiny, child-sized pen-knife. As I studied it, I realized that it was identical to the small knife I was given when I joined Cub Scouts. I was taken aback. Surely such a miniscule knife would be unable to carve significant words in an oak tree. I needed my sturdy Swiss Army knife! But I could find nothing else, and I was sure Manuel had led me here for just this task. So I went to work, picking away at the gnarly tree trunk with my insignificant little knife.

It seemed an impossible task, almost comically unimaginable. But I stuck with it for a long while and realized that, splinter by splinter, I was leaving my "heart mark" on the oak. With more than a tinge of frustration, I kept thinking, "A larger knife could do this so much quicker." Yet, I labored on, sweat dripping into my eyes.

Manuel spoke from beside the next tree where he was watching. "A bigger knife or a power tool would be great about now, huh?"

"Sure would!" I said with more than a hint of irritation in my voice.

He paused, then said, "Morty, our life message is not quickly carved. It is the result of many, many small decisions. It is formed through beliefs and values that are lived out on ordinary days. Your legacy is determined by how you repeatedly handle the truth." Manuel made sense again, but I didn't understand why everything had to be a metaphor. Nevertheless, I worked on. A tenacity to finish drove me on. This was a hard, but a holy journey home.

I carved the words in the box first. When it was finally done, I stepped back to admire my efforts. The simplicity of its message was a bit embarrassing.

Manuel stepped up beside me and read it aloud with a deep and sonorous voice: "Died in love, joy, and peace." He paused a moment to let the words ring, and then said, "I like it. I like it very much!"

The words weren't profound or original, but they were passionate and sincere. I desired to die confident in God's love for me. I also longed to make my death an act of love for God and an expression of great love for all those around me.

After studying my words, Manuel commented, "You know, the Great One saw his death as an act of love for God." He stared harder at the words in the box. "Joy, huh? Death and joy? Are you sure, Morty? That's an unusual combination."

I had thought about this and I was ready. "Yes, sir. I am convinced that, even though death is calling sooner than I wanted, I can meet it with a smile. Sure, it will be frightening to walk through the strangest door of my life. But my focus will be on all the amazing times I have had on this side of the door and all the glorious times I believe I am about to have on the other side. I want to share all those joys with those closest to me."

"And peace is easy," I continued. "I want to say goodbye in a way that imparts the peace of God to others. I want to go out as calmly as a baby falling asleep in a strong Father's arms."

Manuel smiled and said, "Morty, I have to tell you something. If your carving doesn't match reality when it happens, it will disappear and be replaced by a true account. But I truly believe your carving will last."

I thought I would be exhausted after my first carving, but through my pain came the strength of urgency that drove me on. I immediately set to work on the heart—the summary of my life.

I seemed to have mastered the technique and carving went much more quickly the second time. I soon was able to set down the knife to survey my six-word inscription on the tree: "HE LOVED GOD AND OTHERS GREATLY." As I looked at those words, I got excited. I pumped my fist in the air and let out a victory cry, "It is finished!"

Manuel stood beside me. Without looking at him, I blurted, "Well, I'm not a poet, but it's the one thing I want people to say about me at my funeral." Then I added, "I hope it can be said honestly." The silence lingered for at least a full minute. Then I asked, "Any comments, Manuel?"

He didn't say a word, but pointed down the lane. When my gaze followed his finger, I saw a huge, bizarrely shaped oak tree. Some branches pointed up and some reached wide, reminiscent of a cross. A few moments earlier it had not been there at all. Now it stood in the center of the lane as if it ruled the entire reach of trees we had passed through. It was covered with verdant, green leaves, and acorns rained down from its branches. It had no tombstone at its foot.

"Go see what's carved in the middle," Manuel directed.

As I drew close to this Life Tree, I gazed inside its heart. Hewn in large, rough letters were the words, "HE LOVED GOD AND OTHERS PERFECTLY."

Manuel had followed me and looked with awe at the carving. "Morty, to understand the Great One you must understand his heart. This is the mission for which he lived and died. Your inscription is as close to his as you can humanly get. Well done, good and faithful carver!"

After receiving the compliment that felt more like a blessing, I realized that I felt absolutely spent, completely done. I was exhausted and acutely aware of the pain that wracked my entire body. It had spread and intensified in the last few minutes. I slumped under its weight.

Manuel stopped my fall with a shout. "No! Morty, we must travel just a short way further."

"I can't" was all I could muster.

"Yo can!" Manuel assured. "Use your knife to help you walk."

Just as I was about to say "Are you crazy?" the pen-knife grew hot in my hand. I dropped it and watched as it expanded and lengthened. Within sixty seconds it had become a powerful, four-foot broadsword. It was a noble piece of exquisite craftsmanship. Diamonds sparkled on the hilt. The blade was shining hard steel with a razor-sharp double edge.

I stammered, "It's m-m-magnificent! . . . But if it's for me, I just can't fight anymore."

With tenderness, Manuel replied, "You don't have to. Your fighting days are done. Take the sword, not to fight with, but to lean on. It will hold you up for the last short way of our journey. Truth can always be trusted."

I stuck the sword in the ground and leaned on it. The sword held my weight and, as I rested, I felt some relief. Slowly, step by step, with my Sword of Truth as a cane, I followed Manuel out of Legacy Lane.

Stage 7

Reunion River

"Into your hands I commit my spirit"

I hobbled on with Manuel at my side. The shadow over the valley darkened dramatically as the walls loomed together to form a narrow canyon. I leaned on the Sword and took one step at a time, painstakingly repeating the process again and again. Weariness weighed me down. Pain held me in a vise grip. I knew death was near. I kept thinking I would fall down, never to rise again, but somehow I continued on. Breath after breath seemed as though it would be my last, but then I would gasp and breathe again.

I wondered, *What will death feel like? Will it be like nodding off in my recliner in the family room? Will I fall asleep into a brilliant dream that never stops?*

Or will it be like going under water and not being able to swim, unable to pop to the surface to gasp for a breath? Will it feel like being on a roller coaster just before it plunges into free fall?

I had questions, but not yet an answer. Although I longed to rest, I was afraid to stop lest I would never move forward again. Manuel was my guide and inspiration. The Sword was my essential crutch. The end of the valley was my determined destination.

Without warning, the air was rent by an ear-splitting *kee-eeee-arh, kee-eeee-arh*. Although I had by now heard this tormenting screech many times, this was more evil, hate-filled, and closer than any of the others. I jerked my head skyward, and my vision was filled by an enormous Hater Hawk blazing toward me, talons and beak extended for a kill. My mind flashed to the slaughtered rabbit in the meadow, torn to pieces in the blink of an eye.

Something rose within my chest, and for the first time it was not a feeling of panic or helplessness. It was anger and authority mixed in powerful combination. With one sweeping motion, I lifted the Sword above my head and pointed it directly at the hawk as it streaked toward me. The vile thing was so close I could see the shock in its eyes as it realized its fatal mistake. It had no time to change direction; it slammed into my shining Sword, impaling itself on the razor-sharp blade. We both tumbled to the ground.

I was stunned into a moment of unconsciousness, but when I opened my eyes I saw the Hater Hawk give one last gasp and fall silent. A nauseating stench filled the air. Manuel's hand reached down to help me to my feet. A grin spread across his face. "Well done, Amigo! I guess I was wrong...you did have one fight left!"

The adrenalin coursing through my body battled with pain and exhaustion, and I couldn't decide whether to get up or lie there forever. It was the stench that settled my mind. I refused to die next to this foul-smelling fowl. I took Manuel's hand, rose from the ground, and moved ahead.

The shadow cloud had grown so thick that the sky was nearly black. The canyon walls were so close I could literally reach out my hands and touch them both at once. Manuel and I could no longer walk side by side, but moved in single file with him in the lead. Every three steps or so, Manuel would look over his shoulder, making sure that I was still behind him and on my feet.

Manuel began to sing, softly at first, and then with more power. It was a song from another place, a melody like I had never heard before. It was light and dancing, yet solid and robust. It was in a language I had never heard, as if from a distant planet. Yet, otherworldly as the song was, there was something familiar about it. Listening closely, I decided it must be a lullaby from my childhood, but not one I had ever learned. I wondered who had sung it to me.

The longer Manuel sang, the more certain I became that I knew the song—perhaps from infancy, or even the womb. If I'd had breath enough, I would have begged Manuel never to stop singing it. The song lifted my spirit, eased my pain, strengthened me, coaxed me forward, and comforted my fears.

Manuel slowly tapered the volume of his lullaby until it faded completely.

"What was that song?" I asked between gasps.

"That, my beloved friend, is your personal Knitting Song. As you were being knit together in your mother's womb, angels softly sang the instructions to the chromosomes that became you. It is a magnificent song, isn't it?"

"That is amazing," I replied. "It reminds me of a prayer I have sometimes prayed-- 'Lord make me as beautiful as I was in your mind when you first thought about me.'"

"Morty, that is a captivating prayer, worthy of receiving great answers."

The canyon had narrowed so much that I expected to reach a dead-end at any moment. But then, the walls opened abruptly into a river valley. At least, I thought it was a valley; it was now so dark that I could see less than a hundred feet in any direction. I felt sand under my feet. A few yards ahead, I could see a coal-black river flowing swiftly and silently. Something told me that the water was deep.

We stopped on the riverbank and stood in absolute stillness. Manuel didn't need to tell me where we were. I knew this was the end of Shadow Valley.

After a few long minutes, Manuel said, "Morty, it's time to cross."

I hated rivers. I had almost drowned in one when I was five years of age, dragged under by a deceptively swift current. I was not a swimmer and had no desire to be. Now here I stood, trembling as my lifelong fear crept from my toes to overtake my whole, worn body until it seemed to strangle me.

I choked out, "Is this the River of Death?"

"Some may call it that, but we call it Reunion River," Manuel replied.

"B-b-but I can't swim!"

Manuel didn't seem to hear me. He said, "Morty, I have watched over you thus far, haven't I? I am going to be with you all the way through this."

I was comforted by Manuel's reassurance, but the fear did not completely subside. I dug my toes into the sand, trying to grip the earth with the strength I had left.

Manuel counseled, "Morty, let go and let's go. Holding on when it's time to cross is not good for you or for those staying behind."

I recalled my grandfather's death. He had grown worse and worse from the cancer that had invaded his body, yet Grandpa was stubborn and scared to say goodbye. Grandma kept pushing the doctors to do more, to try something else—experiment, do anything to give him a few more days. The result of their obstinance was ugly and undignified. His life was prolonged for another month, but it was a hellacious month for the entire family, not to mention exorbitantly expensive. I realized now that Grandpa had been digging his toes into the sand on the banks of the River. I couldn't blame him, but I didn't want to be like him.

My mind turned to my backpack. There had always been something in it to help me, so now I began once more to explore its magical interior. Perhaps there was a life preserver or even a raft waiting inside.

Manuel watched my fruitless search and then said, "Morty, it's empty. Leave it on the ground. In fact, Morty, I need you to undress and put your clothes beside the backpack. You can't take anything across the River. The only thing you can take further is the Sword."

Fear still clutched at me, but then I remembered my Life Tree carving. *Is this peace and joy? No, it is mistrust.* "I am sorry, Manuel. Forgive me. I trust you!"

I stripped completely naked as Manuel had directed. I was beyond self-consciousness or embarrassment. This wasn't the time for modesty.

I finished letting go of the past and mere possessions, picked up the Sword, and walked the final few steps to the River's edge. I tried to see across to the other bank, but the River was too wide. In the deepening darkness I could see only twenty yards ahead.

Then I heard the lullaby again, my Knitting Song. Manuel wasn't singing it. The melody drifted softly through the darkness from across the water.

"Take my hand and it will be okay," Manuel said.

"Okay, Manuel. I give myself into your hands. Let's cross."

We stepped hand-in-hand from the sandy bank into the River. The water was cool, but not cold. It flowed around us swiftly, but not enough to push us off balance. We waded in to our ankles . . . our knees . . . our waists . . . our chests. I could hear the tender lullaby, but my other senses were filled with nothing but darkness and water.

I began to accept the fact that we would simply walk deeper until we drowned. Strangely, I was hardly afraid. The deeper we waded, the greater the peace that came over me. Then, as the water reached my chin, the current stopped flowing. The River had become a still, ripple-free lake with a surface as smooth as glass. Before I could take it in, a silent crack appeared in the mirrored surface before us. The crevice deepened until it reached the river bottom where we stood. It grew into an aisle wide enough for the two of us to walk hand in hand. We walked forward and deeper, Manuel and I, and the walls of the watery canyon grew until they towered above our heads. All remnants of my fear were transformed into wonderment.

The sound of my Knitting Song began to build in volume and tempo. The mood of the song was changing from comfort to victory. There was a beckoning glow brightening in the distance, and a warm tropical breeze laced with delightful aromas caressed my face. The aromas were reminiscent of roses and night-blooming jasmine.

I realized that I had no pain. My legs, which had felt like cement blocks when we stepped into the River, now began to spring with every step. The Sword, my make-shift cane, became light as a pencil in my hand, and I waved it over my head like a child at play celebrating a great victory.

The glowing light surrounded us and the music grew steadily more grand, noble, and triumphant. Then Manuel began to chuckle, eventually breaking into robust, joy-filled belly laughter.

I could hear cheering that became more exuberant with every step I took. In the radiance ahead, not-yet visible people, or angels, or both, were applauding. They were clapping for Manuel and for me, shouting their glee at our arrival! My heart swelled with such joy that I thought it might burst from my chest.

The shouts rang out from a massive crowd just beyond my view. They sounded like a packed Yankee Stadium when someone hits a grand slam, or like an Olympic Stadium when the marathon winner runs his final lap. Their jubilant cries became distinguishable: "It's the Great One and Morty! They're home! They're home forever! Welcome home! Rejoice!"

I turned to my companion and watched in astonishment as he was transfigured beside me. His glowing countenance radiated a tangible sensation of love in every direction—especially in mine. I stammered, "So y-you are the Great One?"

"I am," he admitted, and he winked at me with his now-familiar smile. "Our hard and holy journey is now done and you are home!"

Then I heard voices I knew, voices of people I loved who were no longer living, at least not on earth. I couldn't wait! I began to run toward the glow. Then, from within the shining light ahead, I heard an authoritative but kind voice call out, "Morty!"

The glowing light began to fade and I felt myself start to awaken. I heard the voice again—"Morty!"—but this time it was more earthly than heavenly. My mind shouted, "No! I never want to wake up." Yet once more, gently and firmly, the voice spoke my name, "Morty."

My eyes opened to see the faces of my pastor, my doctor, and several family members gathered around my hospital bed. My wife had my hand in hers. My pastor's hand was on my shoulder.

"Morty," my pastor said gently, "the doctor tells us you will be going home soon."

I was completely disoriented. I rubbed my eyes, said nothing, and tried to clear my mind. I pondered, *Home? Which home do they mean?* I couldn't speak. *Am I gone or am I here?*

I felt a peaceful smile spread slowly across my face. It didn't matter which home they were referring to. I was fully prepared to die, but just as prepared to really live! I was ready to walk out of that hospital or walk into heaven.

Either way, I knew that it would be a good walk home.

CPSIA information can be obtained at www.ICGtesting.com
Printed in the USA
BVOW11s2051301113

337793BV00001B/1/P